THE LATIN MASS EXPLAINED

"This is My body, which is given for you." —Luke 22:19

THE LATIN MASS EXPLAINED

Msgr. George J. Moorman

Foreword by
Msgr. R. Michael Schmitz
VICAR GENERAL, INSTITUTE OF CHRIST THE KING SOVEREIGN PRIEST

Introibo ad altare Dei.
Ad Deum qui laetificat juventutem meam.

I will go unto the altar of God.
To God, Who giveth joy to my youth.

TAN Books
Charlotte, North Carolina

Imprimatur: Rev. Msgr. David D. Kagan, J.C.L.
Vicar General
Rockford, Illinois
November 16, 2007

The Nihil Obstat and Imprimatur are official declarations that a book or pamphlet is free from doctrinal or moral error. No implication is contained therein that those who have granted the Nihil Obstat or Imprimatur agree with the contents, opinions or statements expressed.

Imprimatur for the
original edition: ✠ Herman J. Alerding
Bishop of Fort Wayne

Originally published circa 1920 by Our Sunday Visitor Press, Huntington, Indiana, as *The Mass: The Eucharistic Service of the Catholic Church.* Retypeset, with many editorial adjustments, including addition of the footnotes, and published by TAN Books in 2007.

ISBN: 978-0-89555-764-3

Front cover: Solemn Pontifical High Mass celebrated by the Most Rev. Raymond L. Burke, Archbishop of St. Louis, at St. Francis de Sales Oratory in St. Louis, Missouri, on the occasion of Confirmations, October 15, 2005.
Back cover: A view of St. Francis de Sales Oratory in St. Louis, Missouri, which is under the care of priests of the Institute of Christ the King Sovereign Priest, who celebrate the "extraordinary form" of the Latin Mass.

Cover design by Milo Persic.

Printed and bound in the United States of America.

TAN Books
Charlotte, North Carolina
www.TANBooks.com

2010

The Prophecy of Malachias

"FOR from the rising of the sun even to the going down, My name is great among the Gentiles, and in every place there is sacrifice, and there is offered to My name a clean oblation: for My name is great among the Gentiles, saith the Lord of hosts."

—*Malachias* 1:11

Foreword

By Msgr. R. Michael Schmitz

FREEDOM is one of the greatest gifts the Almighty has bestowed on man. Through this gift, we are really formed to His image, because among all earthly creatures He gives us the unique opportunity to embrace His will freely, to accept it, and to make it fully ours. The wealth of possibilities this capacity opens to everyone is unfathomable, and it is for this gift that man has been rightly called the crown of creation.

Holy Mother Church is a reflex of this freedom because she is the continuation of the Mystery of the Incarnation and Salvation in this world. Through her, the Redeemer not only re-creates our lost freedom by taking away the slavery of sin, but also blesses us with unending graces to secure a true life of freedom for those of good will. This liberality of God is visible in the liberality of Holy Mother Church, who gratifies her children with all the riches one needs to survive in this poor and spiritually starving world.

Thus, it would seem unnatural to this generous Mother to withhold from us the treasures of beauty and wisdom which, throughout the centuries, have led innumerable of her children to the glory of Heaven. Pope Benedict XVI underscores this truth in the introduction of his Apostolic letter *Summorum Pontificum*: "It is known, in fact, that the Latin liturgy of the

Church in its various forms, in each century of the Christian era, has been a spur to the spiritual life of many saints, has reinforced many peoples in the virtue of religion and fecundated their piety."

Consequently, the freedom of grace of the children of God postulates, from the motherly generosity of the Church, that present and future generations of the faithful should have free and large access to the fullness of the liturgical forms the Holy Ghost has created as an appropriate expression of the glorification that the whole Mystical Body of Christ owes constantly to the Triune God, Creator, Redeemer and Sanctifier of the human race.

Providentially, therefore, and with a gesture of loving largesse after the example of the heavenly Father, the visible Father of Christianity has granted *motu proprio*, of his own initiative, a decree that throws the doors of the liturgical treasury of the Latin Church again wide open for clergy and laity alike. The Holy Father appeals to the wisdom and charity of the Bishops to understand and implement his disposition, which is meant to be a sign of reconciliation inside and outside the Roman Catholic Church. In this intent, it has already borne fruit and received praise and recognition worldwide.

Freedom needs guidance. The liturgical richness of the extraordinary form of the Latin Rite shows in many ways that the sacramental mysteries instituted by Christ are a beginning of the eternal freedom and a glimpse of the glory of Heaven. Hence, in these lands of shadow and sinfulness where human frailty finds a path to the light with great difficulty, Holy Mother Church, under the direction of continuous inspiration from above, has organically developed forms and details to guide our steps to a divine worship that guarantees our contact with the Godhead and at the same time elevates our soul and body to a genuine piety nourished by the grace of Christ.

This is exactly where books like the present one come to play an important role. At all times, the Church has invited both her priests and all her faithful to love and cherish her liturgy. The clergy especially need to have a profound knowledge of the mysteries of which they are called to be the faithful ministers. Those among the laity, however, who have wanted to follow more closely the universal call to holiness have likewise been interested in deepening their knowledge about the theological and ceremonial meaning of the Holy Sacrifice of the Mass. Thus, many approved authors, at different times and under various aspects, have explained the liturgical life of the Church with great expertise. Among the more important were Durandus a Mende, the holy Cardinal Tommasi di Lampedusa, Blessed Dom Marmion, Blessed Cardinal Schuster, the Fathers Sterky, Fortescue, Eisenhofer and Gihr—and many others could be mentioned.

Today, knowledge of the *extraordinary form* of the Latin Rite is not widely spread. Pope Benedict XVI has pointed to the reality of the lack of a general liturgical formation in the letter to the Bishops issued together with the *motu proprio* about the classical liturgy: "The use of the old Missal presupposes a certain degree of liturgical formation and some knowledge of the Latin language; neither of these is found very often." While many of the young clergy and many lay youth are deeply impressed by the classical liturgy which they may happen to discover, few have teachers or literature at hand to be instructed in order to understand even better what they already admire.

The re-publication of an introduction to what is today often called the "Latin Mass" or the "Traditional Latin Mass" is therefore not only most timely, but fills to some extent a gap which needs to be closed at many levels. The present work by Monsignor George J. Moorman, in his time a well-known liturgical scholar with long practical experience, on the one hand contains much detailed explanation of the individual ceremonies and rubrics, but, on the other, remains accessible and clear so that those unfamiliar with the extraordinary form can use the book with profit.

The passages about the theological sense of the concept of sacrifice, the justification of the use of the Latin language, the description of the liturgical vestments and vessels, and the detailed, step by step elucidation of all parts of the Holy Mass, to mention only a few of the many elements of Monsignor Moorman's work, will be most useful to all who want to understand better what happens at the Altar. However, all who desire a more profound faith in the Mystery and the ability to convey their own conviction to others will likewise appreciate the present treatise. While a book like this, given its age and its more general approach, cannot easily embrace all theological and liturgical facts and opinions, and may thus present here and there a more local or personal viewpoint not accepted by all traditional liturgists, it constitutes without doubt a good introduction into the rite of the Holy Sacrifice of the Mass and will be for many a solid base for further studies.

The lay people who read this book may wish to share it with their pastors and their friends among both the older and younger clergy. It should be in the hands of interested seminarians and of altar servers. It will be part of the liturgical revival which the Church so ardently hopes for through the voice of the Roman Pontiff. The liturgy it explains was "never juridically abrogated" and ". . . the Roman Missal promulgated by St. Pius V and reissued by Blessed John XXIII is to be considered as an extraordinary expression of that same 'Lex orandi,' and must be given due honor for its venerable and ancient usage." The more this extraordinary source of liturgical awe is set free for all, the more it will inspire the liturgical life of the Church. One step toward this freedom, springing from knowledge and love, will be this new edition of the notable work of Monsignor George J. Moorman.

Msgr. R. Michael Schmitz
Vicar General,
Institute of Christ the King Sovereign Priest

Author's Introduction

TO Catholics familiar with the Traditional Latin Mass, nothing is more sacred than the Mass. To a person not familiar with the Latin Mass, nothing is more mystifying. "What is going on at the altar?" he asks. It is something so different from everything we meet with in our daily life: the vestments, the altar, the burning candles, the tinkle of the bell, the singing, the language, the ceremonies, the whispered prayers, the awe and reverence of the congregation—what does it all mean?

To those inclined to ridicule, we would advise the reading of Mr. Augustine Birrell's (Protestant) testimony in the *Nineteenth Century* (April, 1896): "There is much that is touching and forlorn in the spectacle of the English Roman Catholic no longer able to adore his Risen Lord in any one of those stately mother-churches built by the piety and still instinct with the genius of his ancestors, or to hear within their walls the tinkle of that bell, a sound carrying with it a richer freight of religious association than any other sound or incident in Christian worship. The Mass is a tremendous mystery, so profoundly attractive, so intimately associated with the keystone of the Christian faith, so vouched for by the testimony of Saints! Nobody today, save a handful of vulgar fanatics, speaks irreverently of the Mass. If the Incarnation be indeed the one divine event to which the whole creation moves, the miracle of the altar may well seem its restful shadow, over a dry and thirsty land, for the help of man, who is apt to be discouraged if perpetually told that everything really important and interesting happened once for all, long ago, in the chill, historic past."

Before entering into an explanation of this great religious ceremony, we feel constrained to give our readers that beautiful picture of the Mass drawn by the pen of Cardinal Newman, who himself was a convert to the Catholic Church:

"Nothing is so consoling, so piercing, so thrilling, so overcoming, as the Mass, said as it is among us. I could attend Masses forever and not be tired. It is not a mere form of words—it is a great action, the greatest action that can be on earth. It is not the invocation merely, but, if I dare use the word, the evocation of the Eternal. He becomes present on the altar in flesh and blood, before Whom angels bow and devils tremble. This is that awful event which is the scope, and is the interpretation, of every part of the solemnity.

"Words are necessary, but as means, not as ends; they are not mere addresses to the throne of grace, they are instruments of what is far higher, of consecration, of sacrifice. They hurry on as if impatient to fulfill their mission. Quickly they go; for they are awful words of sacrifice, they are a work too great to delay upon; as when it was said in the beginning: 'What thou doest, do quickly.' Quickly they pass; for the Lord Jesus goes with them, as He passed along the lake in the days of His flesh, quickly calling first one and then another. Quickly they pass; because as the lightning which shineth from one part of Heaven unto the other, so is the coming of the Son of Man. Quickly they pass;

for they are as the words of Moses, when the Lord came down in the cloud, calling on the Name of the Lord as He passed by, 'The Lord, the Lord God, and abundant in goodness and truth.' And as Moses on the mountain, so we too make haste and bow our heads to the earth, and adore.

"So we, all around, each in his place, look out for the great Advent, 'waiting for the moving of the water.' Each in his place, with his own heart, with his own wants, with his own thoughts, with his own intentions, with his own prayers, separate but concordant, watching what is going on, watching its progress, uniting in its consummation—not painfully and hopelessly following a hard form of prayer from beginning to end, but like a concert of musical instruments, each different, but concurring in a sweet harmony, we take our part with God's priest, supporting him, yet guided by him. There are little children there, and old men, and simple laborers, and students in seminaries, priests preparing for Mass, priests making their thanksgiving; there are innocent maidens, and there are penitent sinners; but out of these many minds rises one eucharistic hymn, and the great Action is the measure and the scope of it." (From *Loss and Gain*).

What poetry, what pathos, what sublimity in the teachings of our Faith! The human mind, left to its own imaginings, has devised nothing comparable to it. If it could be a mere delusion that inspired the liturgies, the cathedrals, the compositions of Palestrina and all the rest—still more, that sustained the martyrs, the tempted, the suffering, the poor, the dying, as the Eucharistic Sacrifice has done; that inspired such lives as those of St. Francis, St. Teresa, and many a hidden saint in the cloister and in the world; and deaths as those of St. Tarcisius and thousands of Christian deathbeds everywhere all the world over, which are manifestly sustained by the power of the Viaticum—if all this were the result of a mistake, what a magnificent mistake!

But when we recall the sixth chapter of St. John's Gospel, the accounts of the Last Supper, especially that by which St. Paul makes his solitary intrusion into the office of Evangelist, and when we think of the place which the Mass has occupied in the tradition and literature and practical life of the Church, no docile Christian mind could escape the conviction that such a mistake is impossible and that nowhere would the daring words of Richard of St. Victor be more applicable than in this impossible hypothesis: "Lord, if there be a mistake, by Thee we are deceived."

But no! The command was given by the Master: "Do this for a commemoration of me." The Mass is the fulfillment of this command. Every Catholic should strive to become familiar with the principal ceremonies and prayers of the Mass so that he may assist at this sublime function with keener interest and greater fervor.

—Msgr. George J. Moorman

Contents

THE LATIN MASS EXPLAINED

"Et antiquum documentum novo cedat ritui."

"The ancient form [of sacrifice]
yields to the new Rite [the Mass]."

—From the *Tantum Ergo*

PART ONE

The Teaching of the Church On the Sacrifice Of the Mass

Chapter 1

The Nature of Sacrifice

The Significance of Sacrifice

When we speak of the **Mass** we usually associate it with **Sacrifice** and speak of it as the **Sacrifice of the Mass.**

The word **sacrifice** is derived from the two Latin words, ***sacer***, meaning "sacred," and ***facere***, "to make." The words "to sacrifice," as quite commonly used, mean to offer something valuable to a person as a token of affection for, or dependence on, that person. If a father gives all he has to enable his children to receive a good education, and himself lives in straitened circumstances, he is said to make a great sacrifice for his children. When a soldier leaves home and country to battle for the defense of his country at the risk of his life and limb, he is said to sacrifice himself for his country. The young missionary who leaves his native land and the comforts of home to preach the Gospel in foreign lands to hostile people is spoken of as making a great sacrifice. And rightly so, for when wealth and life and that which we hold dear are given for a noble purpose, they are rendered sacred.

In this same sense our offerings made to God may be called **sacrifices.** The poor widow who, out of love for God, cast into the treasury her last mite, made a great sacrifice for God's sake.

It is man's duty to **honor** his fellow men. Some among them—for example, parents, teachers and superiors—must be honored in a special manner. This honor may be shown **interiorly** by respecting them, thinking well of them; but these sentiments are given outward expression—for example, by saluting them, speaking well of them—and thus we show them **exterior** honor. But when we wish to honor a person in a particular manner we offer him a gift, or make him a present. Thus, in the days of feudalism, when the lord visited his domains, the inhabitants offered him presents in order to testify that they acknowledged him as their master. They honored him as their lord.

But God is our **Supreme Lord.** We belong to Him with body and soul. We are subject to Him in all things. Hence, we must give greater honor to God than to all men. We honor God **interiorly** by thinking reverently of Him, by submitting ourselves to Him. We honor God **exteriorly** by showing our reverence and submission outwardly, for example, by words, prayers, etc. If we show respect even toward men not only by word, but especially by visible gifts, how much more should we also honor by gifts God, Who is the Author of our being, to Whom belong Heaven and earth and all things!

Sacrifice as an Act of Divine Worship

There is, however, a wide difference in the manner in which we offer a gift to man and to God. By offering gifts to men, we do not pay them the same honor which we pay to God. When we offer God a gift, we recognize Him as our Supreme Master, to Whom we belong entirely; we do Him the greatest honor—we **adore** Him. The gifts which we offer to men are simply **presented,** but the gifts which we offer to God are **destroyed.** The destruction of the object renders its recovery impossible.

When, of old, the Jews offered a lamb, they brought it to the Temple; then it was slaughtered by the priest, the blood was spilled, and the dead animal was burned. If the offerer had merely **given** the lamb, he would have declared only: "The lamb belongs to God; and not only the lamb, but **all that I possess,** I have from God, and I would give it to Him if He desired it." By the **killing and burning** of the lamb another sentiment is expressed: "God is Master over the life and death of this lamb, over the **life and death of all creatures,** and also over my life. I ought, properly speaking, to give up my life to God; but as God does not demand this, I now give Him, instead of my life, the life of this lamb, and thus show that I am ready, if He so desires, to give up also my life for Him."

As the gifts, or sacrifices, which we offer to God confer the highest honor and are signs of **adoration,** such sacrifices can be offered only to God.

Religious Sacrifice Honors God as God

What, then, is a sacrifice in the sense of divine worship? **A sacrifice is that highest act of religion in which a duly authorized person offers to God some sensible* thing which is visibly immolated,** either physically or mystically, in acknowledgment of God's dominion over all things and of our total dependence on Him.**

He who sacrifices is called a **priest;** the sensible

* Sensible—perceptible to the senses.
** Immolated—killed as a sacrificial victim.

thing which is sacrificed is called the **victim;** the place where it is sacrificed is the **altar.** These four—**priest, victim, altar, and sacrifice**—are inseparable. Each one of them calls for the others.

The intention of a sacrifice may be to give honor to God, to give thanks to Him, to ask a favor, or to make atonement. The offering of a sacrifice gives outward expression to the sentiments of the heart. The man who has a due knowledge of God will be filled with sentiments of respect, of gratitude, of confidence, and of contrition. Since it is part of man's nature to manifest outwardly what he feels inwardly, he will give expression to these sentiments by the offering of some object that he values. If he who offers a sacrifice has no other purpose than to honor God, we call this a **sacrifice of praise.** But if, besides this object, he has the particular intention to thank God, he offers a **sacrifice of thanksgiving.** When the offerer wishes anything particular from God, he offers a **sacrifice of petition.** If he wishes to pacify God, Whom he has offended by sin, he offers a **sacrifice of atonement.**

The man who believes in God understands perfectly that he is bound in conscience to spend his life in serving God, nay, that God is worthy even to be honored by the sacrifice of his life. Man gives expression to these sentiments of the heart by offering sacrifice. For the sacrifice of his own life, he substitutes the offering of other sensible objects. By destroying or otherwise changing them, he acknowledges by this destruction or change of sensible things that God is Sovereign Master of life and death; he states that, were God to require it, he would be willing even to sacrifice his own life in order thus to render Him an honor and homage of which He alone is worthy.

Sacrifice Answers the Craving of Human Nature

Sacrifice is the highest form of religious worship. It is the outward expression of man's entire dependence upon God. This absolute dependence of man upon his Creator is expressed in the destruction, or change, of the thing offered. Without this **destruction**, or **change**, it would seem that man did not fittingly express his interior acknowledgement that God was the Sovereign Master of life and death and, as such, worthy even of being honored by the sacrifice of man's life, were He to require it.

Man instinctively manifests his inward feelings by words and actions. The child, already at a tender age, shows its attachment and affection for its mother by outward signs. The highest, holiest, noblest and strongest sentiments of the soul conscious of its relations to God are those of the supreme adoration due to Him. Now the only outward sign which represents these sentiments of itself is **sacrifice.** Every other outward rite or act of religion may of itself be used to manifest the lower reverence paid to creatures as well as the high worship which is God's inalienable right. We may bow, kneel, prostrate ourselves before creatures, as the subject in the Orient does before the monarch's throne. We may burn incense, as did the Jewish priests before the ark of the covenant, or utter "the harmony of sweet sounds" in honor of the Saints and Angels. Take away sacrifice, and religious worship has no outward sign which by itself expresses those high sentiments toward the Ruler of the Universe which are the most obligatory on mankind.

Chapter 2

Sacrifice Before the Time of Christ

Sacrifice in the Patriarchal Age

It is natural for man to believe in a Supreme Being. It is also natural for him to give expression to the sentiments entertained toward the Ruler of the Universe. Hence we find that the custom of offering sacrifice to the Deity is as old as the human race. On the initial page of history we read how Cain and Abel, the sons of Adam, offered sacrifices to the Lord: the one offering the fruits of the field, the other immolating the firstlings of the flock. So also, when the waters of the Deluge had subsided and Noe stepped forth from the ark, his first act was to offer holocausts to God in thanksgiving for his own and his family's preservation. Sacrifices were offered by Abraham, Job, Melchisedech and all religious-minded men who lived in the Patriarchal age before the law of God was promulgated on Mt. Sinai.

Sacrifice among the Pagans

The Gentile nations themselves, "seated in the valley and shade of death," did not lose every ray of the primal revelations and usages. With the notion of a Supreme Being, they preserved universally the practice of sacrifice, a fact which goes far to show that sacrifice was according to the heart of man's rational nature. Among all tribes and nations of whom history has left us any record, we find the two mysterious institutions, sacrifice and priesthood. This is so universally true that the Greek historian Plutarch, who lived in the second century before Christ, did not hesitate to say: "You may find cities without walls, without literature, and without the arts and sciences of civilized life, but you will never find a city without priests and altars, or which does not have sacrifices offered to the gods."

There is in man a religious instinct by reason of which he reaches out spontaneously in thought and affection to the God Who made him. There is also within man a natural tendency to express his religious sentiments by the sacrifice of something that is dear to him and thus show outwardly his total dependence on the Author of his being.

Sacrifice, therefore, was even under the Law of Nature, and among the Patriarchs, from the beginning of the world, the essential form of religion. That these sacrifices, when offered with the proper dispositions of the heart, were agreeable to the Almighty, we may gather from Holy Scripture, which tells us that "the Lord had respect to the offerings of Abel." (*Gen.* 4:4). From the very fact that God showed His pleasure in such sacrifices, we are naturally led to believe that He Himself had taught men, even from the beginning, to worship Him in this manner. However, this original revelation concerning sacrifice, traces of which are found among all nations, became very much corrupted in the course of time. In order, therefore, to teach men how to worship Him properly, God chose a particular people to whom He gave express and minute directions about the sacrifices that they were to offer.

Sacrifice among the Chosen People

This chosen people was the Jewish nation. When Jahweh manifested Himself amid thunder and lightning on Mt. Sinai and delivered to Moses the written law engraved on tablets of stone, He also prescribed the sacrifices which He was pleased to accept from the people of His choice. (*Num.* 28). Out of this nation God chose a particular family—that of Aaron—to offer these sacrifices. These sacrifices were of various kinds. In some the victim was only partially consumed by fire, in others, entirely.

God Himself prescribed most minutely all the rites and ceremonies to be observed in that most solemn act of public worship. (*Lev.* 1 ff.). Sacrifice was not only the essential worship of the entire nation, it was also the essential worship of each individual. Whenever an Israelite committed a sin he was bound by the law of God to confess that sin and to offer sacrifice. (*Lev.* 4). The sinner led to the priest the animal destined for sacrifice. He then laid his hand upon the head of the victim, in order to acknowledge before God that this innocent animal was intended to bear his sins and to die in his place. The animal was then slain by the priest, and its blood was poured round about the altar. By this the sinner acknowledged that God was worthy to be honored by the sacrifice of his own life, especially after having offended Him so grievously by sin.

Many and various as were those sacrifices, comprising the fruits of the earth and the firstlings of the flocks, they all clustered around one which was par excellence the sacrifice of the Old Law: the immolation of the Paschal Lamb, which commemorated the deliverance of Israel's firstborn from the sword of the destroying angel in Egypt. Every year, on the tenth day of the first month, the head of each family was to procure a male lamb of that year, free from all blemish and defect. Four days later, at the same hour in every house, the lamb was sacrificed with the greatest care, so that no bone was broken. Then it was roasted on a fire and served with unleavened bread. The Israelites were to eat it in haste, having their loins girt, shoes on their feet, and holding staves in their hands; for it was the **Phase,** that is, the Passing or **Passover** of the Lord. (*Exodus* 12). The Sacrifice of the Paschal Lamb was not only commemorative of a past deliverance. It also symbolized a future redemption. It was the **type** (prefigurement) of another Sacrifice, in which the Immaculate Lamb of God was to be immolated on the altar of the Cross, for the redemption of the human race from the death of sin and for the deliverance of mankind from the yoke of Satan.

Need of a Perpetual Sacrifice

As sacrifice was instituted by God Himself in the very beginning of the world for the most sacred ends, it was never to cease. The continual, daily sacrifice ordained by God Himself was kept up until the coming of the Redeemer. As long as the Temple remained, the fire on the altar was never extinguished (*Lev*. 6:13), the blood of victims never ceased to flow, the smoke of sacrifices went up continually to God as a testimony of the people's loyalty to Him Who said: "I am the Lord, thy God," and as a pledge of their hope in the Redeemer,

Who would sacrifice Himself for the sins of the world.

Here, then, we have the cravings of our rational nature, the morally universal practice of mankind, and the sanction of God—all in favor of sacrifice. The number of those who abolished the sacrificial rite weighs only as a little dust in the scale against the countless generations who have used it as the only adequate and worthy means of worshipping God.

Chapter 3

The Sacrifice of the Cross

The Sacrifices of the Old Law Were Symbolic

Sacrifices were offered to God at all times. On the very threshold of Paradise we see the smoke of sacrifice ascending to Heaven. Sacrifices were offered by all nations, as Plutarch says: "You will never find a city which has not sacrifices offered to the gods." Sacrifice was ordained by God Himself. Bloody sacrifices were offered to keep before the mind of man the remembrance of his dependence upon Divine Providence; of his sinfulness, in consequence of which he was deserving of death; and of the promise of a Redeemer, Who by the shedding of His blood was to atone for sin.

The victim which was slain represented the sinner. By immolating the victim, the sinner publicly acknowledged that by his sins he deserved death. The victim also represented the Divine Victim, Who by His death would make satisfaction for sin. These blood sacrifices served to prepare mankind for the better things which would be revealed through the Redeemer. They were emblems or reminders of the future Great Sacrifice.

We use the crucifix as a reminder of Christ's great Sacrifice on the Cross. It refers to a **past event.** The sacrifices offered before Christ came into the world were also figures, or reminders, of Christ crucified.

They pointed **in advance** to His death, they showed men that He would come and die. From the Sacrifice on Calvary they derived all their merit. To this they gave way when that Sacrifice became an accomplished fact, just as the shadows must fade and disappear before the radiance of the noonday sun.

Because Symbolic, They Were Abolished

Our reason tells us that all the blood of sheep and oxen that was ever shed could not of itself render satisfaction to God for the sins committed by mankind. "For it is impossible," says St. Paul, "that sin should be taken away with the blood of oxen and goats." (*Heb*. 10:4). The blood of sinless animals could atone for sin only in as far as the sacrificing of these animals was ordained by God, represented the intentions of the human heart, and symbolized the Precious Blood of the promised Redeemer.

When the reality appeared, it put to flight the figure. The time came when the many and varied sacrifices of the Old Law were no longer agreeable to God. Wherefore, when the Anointed of the Lord came into the world, He addressed the God of Hosts: "Sacrifice and oblation Thou wouldst not, but a body Thou hast fitted to Me: Holocausts for sin did not please Thee . . . Then said I: behold, I come to do Thy will, O God, that Thou mayest take away the first, and establish that which followeth." (*Heb.* 10:5-9). This was as if He had said: I come to offer Myself an acceptable sacrifice for the sins of the world.

"Look humbly upward; see His will disclose,
The forfeit first, and then the fine impose,

A mulct thy poverty could never pay
Had not Eternal Wisdom found the way,
And with celestial wrath supplied the store—
His justice makes the fine, His mercy quits the score."

The prophetic rites and sacrifices of the Old Law were fulfilled by Christ's Sacrifice on the Cross. The prophecy of Malachias announcing the abolition of the Jewish sacrifices was fulfilled: "I have no pleasure in you, saith the Lord of Hosts, and I will not receive a gift of your hand." (*Mal.* 1:10).

The Sacrifice of the Cross, A True Sacrifice

The great Sacrifice of the New Law is the Son of God Himself, Who by His death on the Cross offered Himself to His Heavenly Father for our sins. St. Paul teaches that Christ offered Himself as a Sacrifice on the Cross when, in reference to the shedding of His blood, he says that Christ "offered Himself unspotted unto God." (*Heb.* 9:14). Christ's death on the Cross was in every sense a true sacrifice. On the Cross we find the essentials of a true sacrifice: **priest, victim,** and **immolation.** At this sacrifice Christ is the **priest,** because He offered it. He is the **victim**, because He was offered. He **immolates** Himself by freely delivering Himself into the hands of His executioners. His Will thus became operative in the external slaying.

Only this sacrifice properly honored God. Who offered it? The Son of God: He with whom God is well pleased. What did He offer? A gift truly worthy of God, a divine gift: Himself. In this sacrifice we see the Redemption of man, the reconciliation of earth with Heaven. On

Calvary, justice and mercy met and kissed. With this Sacrifice, prophecies have passed away, but memorials begin. As the former looked forward to Christ, so shall the latter look back to Him. And now, "this man offering one sacrifice for sins, for ever sitteth on the right hand of God." (*Heb.* 10:12).

Was All Sacrifice to Cease with the Death of Christ?

The Sacrifice of the New Law is Jesus Christ, Who, by His death on the Cross, offered Himself to His Heavenly Father for us. He offered His life in sacrifice but once in this manner. This **redeeming** sacrifice was offered once: "Christ was offered once to exhaust the sins of many." (*Heb.* 9:28). This **redeeming** sacrifice was not, is not, and can not be repeated.

Was this then the end of sacrifice? No, for in the New Law there was to be **a perpetual sacrifice.**

The offering of sacrifice is the best and most excellent manner of honoring God. If Christianity had no sacrifice, the Christian religion would be imperfect, for sacrifice is the only adequate, visible expression of that supreme adoration due to God. Christianity, without sacrifice, would be inferior in its worship to the patriarchal religion. The perfection of the Christian religion demands sacrifice. Christianity, being perfect in all other respects, must have an equally perfect external worship.

But Christianity has the sacrifice of the Cross! Does that not suffice? Yes, as a **redeeming** sacrifice, but not as a **continuing** sacrifice, unless we suppose it to be perpetuated. The Cross is the **atoning** or **redeeming** sacrifice, and, as such, it is as much the property of the Mosaic as of the Christian religion. But reason tells us there must be a **continual** sacrifice. Christians must also have a substantial sign of the homage they owe and ought to pay to God, and which will last as long as the religious worship of which it is the perfection and the crown. If sacrifice were only useful as the price of our ransom from sin, then "the one Sacrifice once offered" would suffice. Then there would be no necessity for **continuing** sacrifices. But sacrifice is useful and required for other purposes: to praise God, to thank Him, to petition Him, to represent continually that which was once accomplished on the Cross and to apply the fruits of it to our souls.

Reason demands a perpetual sacrifice for the perfection of Christian worship. Holy Scripture, too, speaks of a continuing sacrifice which would apply individually to us the fruits of the redeeming Sacrifice and would in this sense be its perpetuation.

God foretold by the Prophet Malachias that a true sacrifice was to be offered to Him throughout the whole world. "I have no pleasure in you, saith the Lord of Hosts: and I will not receive a gift of your hand. For from the rising of the sun even to the going down, My name is great among the Gentiles, and **in every place** there is **sacrifice**, and there is **offered** to My name a **clean oblation**." (*Mal.* 1:10-11). This oblation* can only be the Sacrifice of Christ, for only this is all pure and holy and pleasing to God. But is the prophesied sacrifice perhaps the sacrifice on the Cross? No; for that was offered only in one place, on Mt. Calvary, and on one day; while the new sacrifice

* Oblation—an offering, particularly the act by which the victim of a sacrifice is offered to God.

is to be offered in all places and at all times.

David in his 109th Psalm and St. Paul in the 7th chapter of his letter to the Hebrews call Christ "a priest forever according to the order of Melchisedech." These words indicate that Christ will **always,** to the end of the world, offer a sacrifice similar to Melchisedech's. Christ is called a priest. The chief office of a priest is **to offer sacrifice.** He is called a priest **forever.** It is hereby shown that Christ will always offer a sacrifice. He is called a priest **according to the order of Melchisedech.** But an offering under the appearance of bread and wine was the characteristic of Melchisedech's priesthood. (*Gen.* 14). Do these words refer to Christ's sacrifice on the Cross? No; for there He suffered but once. There He sacrificed in a bloody manner.

Before the coming of the Redeemer there existed two distinct kinds of sacrifice—the bloody, or the sacrifice of animals, and the unbloody, or the sacrifice of bread and wine or the fruits of the earth. Christ offered up Himself under the appearances of bread and wine according to the rite of Melchisedech at the Last Supper. On the following day He offered Himself in a bloody manner on Calvary. Thus did He unite the two kinds of sacrifice of the Old Law in the one adorable sacrifice of His Body and Blood which He offered up under the appearances of bread and wine at the Last Supper.

Bearing in mind, therefore, that the offering of sacrifice is dictated by man's very nature and that, by a divine ordinance, the sacrifices of the Old Law were to be abolished and were to be succeeded by the oblation of a clean (pure and sinless) victim in every place from the rising of the sun even to the going down, we necessarily conclude that the Christian religion, which is but the completion and perfection of all true religion that existed before Christ,* must also have its sacrifice, wherein there is immolated a victim that is dear to man and acceptable to God.

* Cf. the words of the Council of Trent: "This [the Mass], in fine, is that oblation which was prefigured by various types of sacrifices, during the period of nature and of the law; inasmuch as it comprises all the good things signified by those sacrifices, as being the consummation and perfection of them all." (Session XXII, Chap. I).

Chapter 4
The Sacrifice of the Mass

The Mass Is the Perpetual Sacrifice

The Christian religion was established by the self-immolation of a Divine Victim on the altar of the Cross. As long as this perfect religion endures, it must have an altar upon which the Almighty is adequately honored; and we have seen that Calvary's Victim was to be repeatedly offered (in an unbloody manner) until the end of time. For this Victim alone is a clean oblation ever acceptable to God. It alone has power to propitiate God's offended Majesty, and thus to supplant the sacrifice of the Old Law. It alone can be pointed to as a **fulfillment of Malachias' prophecy:** "For from the rising of the sun even to the going down, My Name is great among the Gentiles, and in every place there is sacrifice, and there is offered to My Name a clean oblation." (*Mal.* 1:11). For this reason the Christians of today must be able to say with the Christians of St. Paul's day: "We have an altar." (*Heb.* 13:10). If there be an altar, there must be a sacrifice. This sacrifice, in order to be pleasing to God, must be no other than the sacrifice of Christ Himself; and this sacrifice, the Catholic Church teaches, exists in the Mass.

The Mass Is a True Sacrifice

"The Mass, according to Catholic doctrine, is a commemoration of the Sacrifice of the Cross, for as often as we celebrate it, 'we show the death of the Lord until He come.' (*1 Cor.* 11:26). At the same time, it is not a bare commemoration of that other Sacrifice, since it is also **itself** a true sacrifice in the strict sense of the term. It is a true sacrifice because it has all the essentials of a true sacrifice: its Priest, Jesus Christ, using the ministry of an earthly representative; its Victim, Jesus Christ, truly present under the appearances of bread and wine; its sacrificial offering, the mystic rite of Consecration. And it commemorates the Sacrifice of the Cross because while its Priest is the Priest of Calvary, its Victim the Victim of Calvary and its mode of offering a mystic representation of the blood-shedding of Calvary, the end also for which it is offered is to carry on the work of Calvary, by pleading for the application of the merits consummated on the Cross to the souls of men." (Herbert Cardinal Vaughan, *Vindication of the Bull on Anglican Orders,* 1898).

The immolation of the victim which takes place in the Mass, and which is essential for every true sacrifice, is explained in Chapter 5 under the heading: "The Immolation in the Mass." (See p. 36).

The Mass Was Instituted by Christ

The Mass was instituted by Christ at the Last Supper, on the first Holy Thursday. The first Holy Sacrifice of the Mass was celebrated on the eve of the Passion. Of course, Jesus did not use the same prayers and ceremonies that the priest employs today when celebrating Mass. But in the principal parts, Jesus did precisely what the priest does today. He took bread and wine, blessed it, and consecrated it.

The action of Our Lord at the Last Supper was a **real sacrifice**. There He offered Himself in an unbloody manner: "This is my body, which **is given for you.**" (*Luke* 22:19). "This is the chalice, the new testament in my blood, which **shall be shed** [Greek: which is shed]* **for you."** (*Luke* 22:20). Our Lord speaks of the present, not only of the future. The "shedding of blood" or "pouring out of blood" took place there and then, in a mysterious manner. And He commanded His Apostles to do as He had done: "Do this"—that is, the same thing that I have done: Do ye also change bread and wine into My Body and Blood and offer it to the Heavenly Father. (*Luke* 22:19; *1 Cor*. 11:24). Christ therefore commanded His Apostles thenceforth to celebrate the Mass. When Our Lord said: "Do this for a commemoration of me" (*Luke* 22:19), He made Himself a perpetual Victim, even as He was already a Priest according to the order of Melchisedech. This St. Paul clearly indicates when he says: "For as often as you shall eat this bread, and drink the chalice, you shall show the death of the Lord, until He come." (*1 Cor.* 11:26).

The Mass, a Memorial

The unbloody sacrifice was, in the first place, to be a memorial of Christ's bloody sacrifice. Monuments are erected to commemorate great events. The greatest event

---

* A footnote in the Greek/Latin (Vulgate) New Testament (Imprimatur 1955) states that the Greek for "shed" in *Luke* 22:20 can be translated as either "is shed" or "shall be shed." Cf. also J. Pohle, "The Mass," in *The Catholic Encyclopedia*, Imprimatur 1911, Vol. X, pp. 9-10.

in human history is man's Redemption. What more natural than that Christ should have left to His followers a perpetual memorial of this prodigy! It is now two thousand years since our Blessed Saviour died upon the Cross for us. Our Lord knew well that men are apt to forget favors, especially those of the distant past. What a contrast between "Hosanna to the Son of David." and "Away with this man. Crucify Him!" What a contrast between spreading their garments in the way before Him, and stripping Him of His garments, casting lots for them, and vesting Him with the scarlet cloak of mockery! What a contrast between the strewing of palm branches where He passed, and platting a crown of thorns for His head! What a contrast between "King of Israel" and "We have no king but Caesar!" Our Lord knew this fickleness of the human mind and heart. And hence, lest we should forget, He said: "Do this in remembrance of Me." Hence, as often as we eat this bread, and drink the chalice, we show the death of the Lord. Therefore St. Thomas says: "In this unbloody Sacrifice we have an abridgment of all His wonders and a standing monument of all His prodigies."

A Channel of Grace

The Mass is not only a **memorial** of the bloody sacrifice on Calvary, it is, in the second place, a **channel of grace**. Christ merited all graces and blessings for us by His death on the Cross. These merits form an inexhaustible fountain whose pure, spiritual waters nourish the supernatural life of the souls (and of those souls only) to which the same are applied. For this reason Jesus not only merited all graces for us but also established certain channels whereby these graces are communicated to us. These channels are the Sacraments and the Sacrifice of the Mass.

But St. Paul tells us emphatically that Christ on the Cross redeemed all people for all times in that He "by His own Blood, entered once into the holies, having obtained eternal redemption." (*Heb.* 9:12). St. Paul, indeed, spoke thus. But this does not mean that man is suddenly, and without the co-operation of his own will, brought back to the state of innocence enjoyed by our first parents before the fall. It does not mean that man is set above the necessity of working to receive for himself the fruits of Redemption. Otherwise children would be in no need of Baptism; there would be no need of a Church. The completion spoken of by St. Paul can therefore refer only to the *objective* side of Redemption, which does not dispense with, but on the contrary requires, the proper *subjective* dispositions. The Sacrifice once offered on the Cross filled the infinite reservoirs to overflowing with healing waters, but those who thirst after justice* must come and draw out what they need to quench their thirst.

We acknowledge that all the merits of the Redemption of mankind are derived from the death of the Son of God. When, therefore, in the celebration of the Divine Mysteries we say, "We offer to Thee this Holy Victim," we do not mean by this oblation to present to God a new payment of the price of our salvation, but to offer to Him on our behalf the merits of Jesus present, and that infinite price which He once paid for us upon the Cross.

How unjust, then, is the reproach that the Mass obscures the Sacrifice of the Cross! Would it not be

* Justice—That is, righteousness, holiness. This is given to the soul by Sanctifying Grace, supernatural Life.

absurd to say that to desire Baptism would be to place one's confidence in water instead of in the blood of the Redeemer and would thus be a disparagement to the merits of Christ? It is just as absurd to say that Catholics, by the daily Sacrifice of the Mass, obscure the glory of the Sacrifice of the Cross and detract from its dignity; since we, by this very means, only *participate in the Sacrifice of the Cross.* Far from derogating from the Sacrifice of Calvary, the Mass only brings it nearer to us and renews and extends its effects in us in a wonderful manner.

The Sacrifice on the Cross is the one Sun that gives life, light and warmth to everything; the Sacraments and the Mass are only the planets that revolve around the central body. Take the Sun away, and both the Mass and Sacraments are annihilated. On the other hand, without the Mass and the Sacraments, the Sacrifice on the Cross would reign as independently as, conceivably, the sun without the planets. Far are we then from believing that anything is wanting to the Sacrifice on the Cross. We regard this sacrifice as so fully sufficient that whatever is afterwards added has been instituted to celebrate its memory and to apply its merits and powers. It is the express **teaching of the Church** (Council of Trent, Session XXII, Chap. I) that the Mass is in its very nature a "commemoration" and an "application" of the Sacrifice of the Cross. The work of sanctification which was begun on Calvary is thus continued and completed on the Christian altar. On Calvary was wrought the Redemption of fallen man; on our altars is promoted the personal sanctification of those already redeemed. On Calvary were merited the graces that make salvation possible; on our altars these graces are offered to the faithful soul.

Chapter 5

The Relation of The Sacrifice of the Mass to The Sacrifice of the Cross

The Sacrifice of the Mass Is the Same as The Sacrifice of the Cross

St. Paul says that Christ offered Himself but once. (*Heb.* 7:27). Christianity has **but one sacrifice**, which is the redeeming Sacrifice **once** accomplished on the Cross. If the Mass is a true sacrifice, then it must be the **same** as the Sacrifice on the Cross. It **is** the same, because there is a numerical identity in the Priest offering the two sacrifices and because there is a numerical identity in the Divine Victim which is offered; and thus, in all that is essential to sacrifice, a Priest and a Victim, the two Sacrifices are essentially **one and the same**. It is the same One Who offers the sacrifice—Jesus Christ. He offers the same gift—His Body and Blood. He offers it to the same One—His Heavenly Father. He offers it for the same ends—to honor and appease God, to impart to us graces. He does this not to redeem us again, not to acquire new graces for us—this He did on the Cross—but in order that the Father, on account of His death, may give us the graces which He merited.

The Sacrifice of the Mass, therefore, is the very same

in all essentials as the Sacrifice of the Cross. That which properly belongs to a sacrifice is the same in both. We have the same Priest in both—Jesus Christ. We have the same Victim in both—Jesus Christ. The **manner of offering,** that is, the way in which Jesus offers Himself, is different.

"In this divine Sacrifice of the Mass," says the Council of Trent, "the same Christ is contained and is immolated in an unbloody manner, Who on the altar of the Cross offered Himself once in a bloody manner. It is one and the same Victim, the same Christ offering Himself by the ministry of the priest, Who then offered Himself on the Cross, the manner of offering alone being different." (Session XXII, chap. II).

CHRIST IS THE PRIEST

The Mass is the same as the Sacrifice of the Cross because the priest is the same in both. According to universal belief, a priest is one who is appointed to stand between God and the people. He has to discharge two orders of duty—the one toward God, the other toward men. He is appointed to offer up that supreme act of public and external worship which is due to God alone and consists of sacrifice. He has positive duties toward men. He is bound to teach and instruct them in whatever relates to the salvation of their souls.

Our Lord is a Priest in the full and literal sense of the term. The description of the priesthood given by St. Paul is strictly verified in Jesus Christ: "For every high priest taken from among men, is ordained for men in the things that appertain to God, that he may offer up gifts and sacrifices for sins." (*Heb.* 5:1). By whom was He ordained to stand as a priest between

God and man? No human hand was ever imposed upon His head, no earthly unction was ever poured over Him. Neither did He "take the honor to Himself"—for "Christ also did not glorify Himself, that He might be made a high priest: but He that said unto Him: *Thou art My Son, this day have I begotten Thee.* As He saith also in another place: *Thou art a priest for ever, according to the order of Melchisedech."* (*Heb.* 5:4-6).

During the three and thirty years of Our Lord's life, the Altar of the Crucifixion was never for an instant out of sight. He yearned for the accomplishment of the sacrifice. On the eve of His death, as Legislator and Priest, He instituted for all time and offered for the first time the Unbloody Sacrifice, the Sacrifice of the Mass; then He forthwith went out to offer the same Sacrifice of Himself in a bloody manner upon the Cross.

Christ the Only Priest

There now exists but One Priest, One Victim, One Sacrifice, One Altar. Are there, then, today no priests? Christ has no succession of priests offering in their own right their own sacrifices, as in the Old Testament. But those who are rightly ordained partake of **Christ's Priesthood,** receiving that certain but limited communication of His power which He is pleased to give. It is not their own, but **Christ's** priesthood that they receive and exercise. Hence they are called Christ's ministers, signifying that when they teach, absolve and offer sacrifice, they are discharging Christ's sacred sacerdotal (priestly) office.*

* The Catholic priest is called an *alter Christus,* an *other Christ.*

Christ a Priest Forever

Being a Priest **"forever, according to the order of Melchisedech"** (*Heb.* 5:6), Our Lord must, in some way or other, offer during all time the sacrifice of which Melchisedech's was the *type.* Now Melchisedech offered a sacrifice of bread and wine. Christ, then, must offer during all time a sacrifice under the appearances of bread and wine. This is what He actually does in the Mass.

He is the Chief Priest and Offerer of the Mass—not simply because He instituted the Sacrifice of the Mass, nor again because its value and graces are derived from Him and depend upon Him alone; but because He alone is perfectly and absolutely **competent** to offer it. Two things are required for the perfect exercise of the sacrificial office: 1) That the act of immolation be within the power of the priest, and dependent on his will. 2) That he himself, having been duly appointed to do so, offer the sacrifice to God.

In the Mass the act of immolation or consecration requires the exercise of Divine power. It is a miracle transcending all human and created power. God has been pleased to employ the Sacred Humanity of the Eternal Son as His instrument for the performance of this stupendous miracle, making Jesus Christ in His Sacred Humanity a sacrificing Priest until the end of time.

Christ, therefore, is the Chief Priest, although He deigned to associate with Himself, as secondary priests or agents, the Apostles and their successors. This He did in order that His Sacrifice might always be **visible;** "Christ Himself," as the Council of Trent declares, "now offering by the ministry of priests." (Sess. XXII, Chap. II).

Hence the words of Consecration are rightly pronounced in **Christ's** name, He being the chief offerer, and not in the name of the secondary offerer who acts as His official agent. "Let a man so account of us as of the ministers of Christ, and the dispensers of the mysteries of God." (*1 Cor.* 4:1). Assuming the person of Christ at the Consecration, the minister does not say: "This is the Body of Christ," but: "This is **My Body.**"

The learned Alcuin, in the eighth century, spoke only the faith of all Christendom when he wrote these words in his *Profession of Catholic Faith:* "Although with bodily eyes I see the priest at the Altar of God offering bread and wine, by the institution of faith and in the pure light of the soul I distinctly see that great High Priest, the Lord Jesus Christ, offering Himself."

CHRIST IS THE VICTIM

The Sacrifice of the Mass is the same as the Sacrifice of the Cross because the Victim is the same in both. The victim is that which is offered. The Victim offered on Calvary was Jesus Christ. The Victim in the Sacrifice of the Mass is the same Jesus Christ. "Who is the priest," says St. Augustine, "but that one Priest Who entered into the Holy of Holies. Who is the priest but that one Priest who was both the **Victim** and the **Priest:** Who, when He found nothing clean and pure enough in this wide world of ours to offer unto God in Sacrifice, offered Himself." (*In Ps.* 132 *et* 26). Because there was nothing in creation capable of rendering to the Divine Majesty an adequate act of adoration, nothing capable of satisfying Infinite Justice for our sins, no victim capable of paying the price of our Redemption, the Son of God assumed a human nature and thus offered Himself. "Sacrifice and oblation [of earthly victims] Thou wouldest not: but a body Thou hast fitted to Me . . . Then said I: behold I come." (*Heb*. 10:5-7).

In order to understand how Christ is the **Victim** in the Sacrifice of the Mass, it will be necessary to know **how He becomes present upon the altar**. The Church teaches that He becomes present through **Transubstantiation**. Transubstantiation is the conversion of the whole substance of the bread into the Body of Christ, and of the whole substance of the wine into the Blood of Christ.

In all objects we distinguish the **substance** and its "accidents," that is, qualities and appearances. The difference between **substance** and **accidents** is easily perceptible in water. A glass of water before our eyes may assume various appearances perceptible to the senses. The water may be **liquid;** it may become **ice;** it may be reduced by means of heat to **vapor.** Thus we behold many changes in the appearances of the water, but its **substance,** that which **stands** ***(stare)*** or lies **under** ***(sub)*** these various appearances remains the same.

We may speak of three different kinds of **conversions** or **changes:**

1) An **accidental** conversion or change, which affects **only the accidents** of a body, e.g., the Transfiguration of Christ on Mt. Tabor;

2) A **substantial** conversion or change, which affects both the **substance and accidents**, e.g., the change of food into blood;

3) A **transubstantial** change or conversion, by which the **substance alone** is converted into another, the accidents remaining the same. Such a change we would have if wood were miraculously converted into iron,

the substance of the iron remaining hidden under the external appearance of wood.

Such a change, faith tells us, takes place at the **Consecration** of the Mass. It is called a **transubstantial** change because it is **beyond**, more than, a substantial change. The Latin word for *beyond* is **trans.**

Christ brought about such a change at the Last Supper. He held bread in His hands. He said: "**This** is My Body." According to Christ's word we have here the conversion of the substance of bread into the substance of Christ's Body, the accidents or appearances of bread, however, remaining. Christ, being God, could work such a change. Having the power Himself, He could give it to others. This He did when He said: "Do this in commemoration of Me." This power, which the Apostles received directly from Christ, is handed down **through the Sacrament of Holy Orders.**

Christ's Two Modes of Existence

When we meditate upon Christ's presence in the Eucharist, the question arises within our minds: **How can Christ be present in Heaven and upon thousands of altars throughout the world?**

Christ has His **natural mode** of existence **in Heaven.** Here all the features and faculties of His sacred body and soul are manifestly glorified in the sight of the Angels and Saints. Such is the indescribable light of glory that flows from the Sacred Humanity that the Heavenly City has no need of the sun to give it light, for the Lamb is the lamp thereof. (*Apoc.* 21). To gaze on Him in His glory, to speak with Him, to be united to Him is to be blessed:

"Joy past compare; gladness unutterable;
Imperishable life and peace and love,
Exhaustless riches and immeasurable bliss."
—*Dante*

But besides this **natural mode** of existence, Our Lord has another, invented by the exhaustless resources of His love at the Last Supper. It is called His **sacramental mode** of existence. At the Last Supper the Apostles beheld Christ both in His **natural** mode of existence and in His **sacramental** mode of existence. In His sacramental manner of existence Christ deigns to dwell in our midst not in the form of man, but under the humble appearances of bread and wine.

Christ does not multiply His Body as many times as there are sacred Hosts. Christ is not multiplied, but the **presence** of Christ is multiplied, that is, His relation to the various Hosts and to their particles.

In nature we find certain objects which astonish us by transgressing almost all the limits of space. Take, for instance, light. Scientists tell us that light moves with a velocity of nearly 186,000 miles per second. In one moment, therefore, light travels a distance more than six times the circumference of the globe. Think of the telegraph and reflect that in a single second the electric current flashes through nearly 300,000 miles of space, ten times the distance around the world. If in the forces of inanimate nature we behold such remarkable phenomena, what may we not expect as possible with regard to the glorified body of Christ? There is absolutely no limit of space or distance for the sacred body of Our Lord. It is present wheresoever the Divine Will decrees.

The presence of Christ's glorified body in so many

Hosts is not unlike that of a thought or idea, which, as soon as it has been expressed by the mouth of a speaker, is instantly in the minds of his hearers.

Therefore we hold: One and the same undivided and not multiplied sacred Body of Our Lord is present under all those forms of bread (that is, those many Hosts) into which it has been called by the all-powerful words of Consecration. And as long as the appearances of bread remain, so long does Christ remain present.

This **sacramental** mode of existence reminds us most forcibly of the Incarnation. By the Incarnation, the Son, "being in the form of God . . . emptied Himself, taking the form of a servant, being made in the likeness of men, and in habit found as a man," and in this condition, without abdicating His Divinity or suffering any loss or diminution of His heavenly glory, humbled Himself to the Sacrifice of the Cross. (*Phil.* 2:6-7). And in like manner every day in the Mass, though being in the form of perfect God and perfect Man and living forever in the infinite bliss of Heaven, without loss or diminution of glory or happiness in either His divine or human natures, He empties Himself under the appearances of bread and wine, and humbles Himself as a Victim to a mystical death on the altar. There is no more astounding miracle than this in the world—and who could believe in it but they who believe in the Incarnation?

The Difference between the Sacrifice of the Cross and the Sacrifice of the Mass

The Sacrifice of the Mass is, under a twofold aspect, identical with the Sacrifice of the Cross. In both sacrifices we have the same **Victim**, Christ Himself,

Who is sacrificed. In both it is the same **Priest** Who sacrifices. For it is Christ, the High Priest of the Sacrifice of the Cross, Who likewise offers the Sacrifice of the Mass through the priest, His representative. The Sacrifice of the Mass **differs** from the Sacrifice of the Cross in the **manner of offering**.

On the Cross the blood of Christ was **really shed,** He really died; while in the Mass there is no real shedding of blood, no real death, but only a **mystical shedding** of blood, a mystical death.

If Jesus were to die again in the Mass, the Sacrifice of the Cross and the Sacrifice of the Mass would not be **one sacrifice**, but **two sacrifices**, and we have seen that there is but **one** sacrifice in the New Law. Besides, Jesus can die no more. His blood was shed on the Cross; it was then really separated from His body. A **real** separation of the Precious Blood from Christ's Sacred Body is no more possible, but **sacramentally** it takes place also on the altar.

In the Mass, Jesus is present under the **separated appearances of bread and wine**. It is true that Jesus is entire—Body and Blood, Soul and Divinity—in the Host as well as in the Chalice, but the **appearance of bread**, which is solid, represents the **Body;** and the **appearance of wine**, which is liquid, represents not the Body, but the **Blood** of Christ. The Sacred Host, therefore, represents to us Christ's body, and the Chalice with the consecrated "wine" represents His blood—consequently, blood separated from the body. But where were body and blood separated? At Christ's bloody death on the Cross. Hence the separated appearances represent the body and blood of Jesus as they were on the Cross when He suffered the bloody death. Christ is, then, present on the altar with the same body that died on the Cross, with the same blood that was shed on the Cross. He is present under **the emblems of the bloody death**, that is, represented as He died on the Cross, when His blood was separated from His body. The Mass is therefore really what Christ intended it to be, a commemoration of Him (cf. *Luke* 22:19), the showing of the death of the Lord. (Cf. *1 Cor*. 11:26).

Being present on the altar in the manner described above, Christ **really** and **truly** offers Himself to His Heavenly Father. For in the Mass He is present in the same manner as at the Last Supper, under the appearances of bread and wine. And there Christ offered Himself in sacrifice, as we learn from the words: "This is My body, **which is given** for you" (*Luke* 22:19); "This is the chalice, the new testament in My Blood, **which shall be shed** for you." (*Luke* 22:20). In Scriptural usage, the words "given for you," "shed for you," are the same as **"offered in sacrifice for you."**

The Immolation in the Mass

The Mass is, therefore, not only a **commemoration** but also a **real immolation**. How is this immolation effected? By the consecrating words: "This is My Body" and "This is the chalice of My Blood . . ." The people see that by the "sword-stroke" of the consecrating words, which are sense-perceptible, Christ is "reduced" from glorious human form to the condition of inanimate matter. There is a vast difference between the appearance of Christ present in His natural form and present under the form of bread and wine. St. John the Apostle describes a vision of Christ in His glory. "I saw," says St. John, "in the midst of the seven golden candlesticks, one like to the Son of man, clothed with a garment down to the feet, and girt about the paps with a golden girdle. And his head and his hairs were white, as white wool, and as snow, and his eyes were as a flame of fire, and his feet like unto fine brass, as in a burning furnace. And his voice as the sound of many waters." (*Apoc.* 1:12-15). With this vision before their minds, the worshippers hearing the words of Consecration, "This is My Body," look at the altar, but the vision is not there; they behold Christ stripped of all beauty and comeliness, of all the appearance of a human being, reduced to the form of bread and wine.

This external change in Christ's mode of existence expresses the signification of a true sacrifice, namely, that God's rule over the human race is so absolute that He deserves that, to satisfy His justice for man's sins, not only the whole race should die, but that even the Divine substitute of infinite dignity should be reduced to inanimate matter.

THE MASS HAS BEEN OFFERED SINCE THE DAYS OF THE APOSTLES

The Mass owes its origin to Christ. The Bible tells us that at the Last Supper Jesus changed bread and wine into His Body and Blood. His intention to offer a real sacrifice on this occasion is expressed in the words: "This is My Body, **which is given** for you" (*Luke* 22:19); "This is the chalice, the new testament in My Blood, **which shall be shed** for you." (*Luke* 22:20). Here we find the fulfillment of the **prophecy of Malachias** foretelling the **"clean oblation"** to be offered **"in every place"** (*Mal.* 1:10-11); here we have the verification of the Psalmist's prediction: "Thou art a priest for ever according to the order of Melchisedech." (*Ps.* 109:4).

Proof from Scripture

When Our Lord had thus offered Himself in sacrifice under the appearances of bread and wine, He commanded His Apostles to do even as He had done: "Do this for a commemoration of Me." (*Luke* 22:19). The Apostles, immediately after the descent of the Holy Ghost, began to celebrate this sacred Rite of the Mass, **"breaking bread** from house to house." (*Acts* 2:46). St. Luke again alludes to the Mass when he tells us that the Christians of Antioch **"were ministering to the Lord."** (*Acts* 13:2). The word **ministering** here used always refers to sacrifice. (Read: *Heb*. 9:21; 10:11). St. Paul, in his letter to the Hebrews, writes: "We [Christians] have an altar, whereof they have no power to eat who serve the tabernacle" (*Heb.* 13:10)—that is, the Jews. An **altar** presupposes a sacrifice. Does the Apostle perhaps mean the Cross? No; for how can we eat of the Cross? He means an altar for offerings, on which food is offered, of which Christians, and only Christians, may eat. Therefore the Christians, **at the time of the Apostles**, had a sacrifice, a holy oblation, of which only the Christians could eat. This can only be the Sacrifice of the Body and Blood of Christ under the forms of bread and wine, the Sacrifice of the Mass.

Proof from Tradition

Tradition, with its hundred tongues, proclaims the perpetual oblation of the Sacrifice of the Mass from the time of the Apostles to our own days.

In the manuscript of the **Didache,** or "The Teaching of the Twelve Apostles," which was written before the year 100, we read: "Being assembled on every Lord's

Day, break Bread and give thanks, after confessing your sins, that your Sacrifice may be a clean one; for it is the Sacrifice of which the Lord has said: In every place, at every time, a clean Oblation shall be offered to My name." (c. 14).

St. Justin, who died about 166, writes: "Of the Sacrifice which we offer in every place, that is, of the Bread and Chalice of the Eucharist, Malachias had prophesied." (*Dial. with Tryph.,* n. 41).

St. Irenaeus, whose master, St. Polycarp, was a disciple of St. John the Evangelist, says: "Christ took that creature bread, and gave thanks, saying: 'This is My body.' And in like manner He confessed the [contents of the] Cup—which, according to us, is a created thing—to be His Blood, and taught the new Oblation of the New Testament; which the Church, receiving from the Apostles, throughout the world offers to God. . . . Respecting which Malachias, one of the twelve Prophets, thus predicted," etc. (*Adv. Haer.* 54, c. 17).

If we consult the **Fathers of the Church,** who have stood like faithful sentinels on the watch towers of Israel guarding the Deposit of Faith, and who have been the faithful witnesses of their own times and the recorders of the past, they will tell us with one voice that the Sacrifice of the Mass is the center of their religion and the acknowledged institution of Jesus Christ. Surely St. Paul, St. Luke, the writer of the *Didache,* St. Justin and St. Irenaeus were better acquainted with the prevailing practices and beliefs of their day than were the so-called reformers of the sixteenth century, and hence they can furnish us with more reliable testimony.

Proof from History

That in the early days of Christianity the Sacrifice of the Mass formed an essential part of divine worship is evident from the fact that the different churches which fell into heresy and separated from Rome during the first five centuries all retained the Eucharistic Sacrifice. The Nestorians and Eutychians who separated from the Catholic Church in the fifth century, and who still exist in Persia (Iran) and in other places of the East, retain to this day the oblation of the Mass in their daily service. So do the Greek schismatics who severed their connection with the Church in the ninth century. With regard to doctrine, some of the early heretics denied that there was only one person in Christ; others, that He had two natures; and others again the primacy of the Bishop of Rome; yet they all were at one in their belief that in the Mass there was offered to God a true sacrifice. That doctrine had been taught so explicitly from the very first that its denial was considered a rejection of Christianity.

It was only when the so-called reformers laid their hands upon the work of God that the Christian altar was overturned, and that the Blessed Eucharist was declared to be merely commemorative bread and wine. Only then was first seen the anomaly of a religion without a sacrifice, a religion without a priesthood—a religion made by man, and wholly inadequate to give due worship to God or to satisfy the needs of human nature.

In view of this, it is not at all surprising that so eminent a scholar as Harnack, the celebrated Protestant theologian of the University of Berlin, should speak in favor of the Catholic form of worship. On the occa-

sion of the Emperor's birthday he delivered a discourse at the university in which he said: "Protestantism has every reason to ask itself whether the new form of worship, which it had to fashion for itself in the sixteenth century in opposition to Catholicism, is altogether sufficient and satisfactory. Is there not in the Catholic Mass an element and a form of adoration to which Protestant worship does not rise? Has not the idea of sacrifice been too much repressed by us?"

PART TWO

The Name, Language and Things Necessary for the Celebration of Mass

Chapter 1

The Name of the Eucharistic Service

How did the great service in the Catholic Church receive the name, **Mass**? The name **Mass** does not occur in the Bible. This, however, does not prove that the Apostles did not celebrate the sacred rite to which we give the name **Mass**. This name is less old than the rite for which it stands. The Apostles, immediately after the descent of the Holy Ghost, began to celebrate this sacred rite which we call the **Mass**, "breaking bread from house to house." (*Acts* 2:46). St. Paul speaks of a Christian **altar:** "We have an altar . . ." (*Heb*. 13:10), and an **altar** is a place of sacrifice.

In a book entitled *The Teaching of the Twelve Apostles* (The *Didache*), which was written before the year 100, we read: "Being assembled on every Lord's day, break Bread and give thanks, after confessing your sins, that your Sacrifice may be a clean one; for it is the Sacrifice of which the Lord has said: 'In every place, at every time, a clean oblation shall be offered to My name.'" These passages show us that the Apostles were obedient to their Master, Who, at the Last Supper, bade them do even as He had done, namely: change bread and wine into His Body and Blood and offer them to God in Sacrifice. They had an altar. They persevered daily in **breaking Bread**.

While Greek was still the popular language at Rome, the name **Eucharist** was given to the service which we call the **Mass**. This name is derived from the two Greek words, ***eu,*** meaning **"good,"** and ***charis,*** meaning **"grace"** or **"gift**." And surely, a better name could not be given to the Sacrament in which Christ gives Himself to us.

When Latin became the universal language of the Roman Empire, the Latin name ***Missa,*** used at first in a vaguer sense, became the exclusive name for the Eucharistic service. The Latin word, ***missa*** or ***missio,*** means a **"dismissal,"** or a **"sending away."**

In the first centuries of Christianity, that part of the Eucharistic service or Mass which preceded the Offertory was called the **Mass of the Catechumens**. Those persons who were being "instructed" in Christian truth before receiving Baptism were called **catechumens**. The Greek word for "instructed" is ***catechumenos.*** From this Greek word we also derive our English words **"catechize"** and **"catechism."** The catechumens were not allowed to be present for the Offertory, Consecration and Communion. They were **dismissed** before the Offertory, and the time of the dismissal was announced by one of the ecclesiastics in the words: ***"Ite, missa est"***—**"Go, it is the dismissal."**

It might be asked: Why were the catechumens not permitted to remain for the entire service? The keeping concealed from those who were not Christians of certain doctrines and practices was called the "Discipline of the Secret." It was based upon the admonition of Christ (*Matt.* 7:6) and was rendered imperative by the persecutions and calumnies against the Church.

That part of the Eucharistic service which followed the dismissal of the catechumens was called the **Mass**

of the Faithful (the Offertory, Consecration and Communion). As there was a dismissal of the catechumens at the end of the first part of the service, so was there a dismissal of the Faithful after the Communion. This dismissal was also announced with the words: ***"Ite, missa est."***

This unessential detail gave its name to the whole service. How the word gradually changed its meaning from dismissal to the whole service is not difficult to understand. To remain *until* the ***missa*** or dismissal of the catechumens, is easily changed into: to remain **for**, or **during**, the ***Missa*** of the Catechumens. When the discipline of the catechumens was done away with, and there was only the one connected service, it was called by the long-familiar name, ***Missa,*** or **Mass**. It is an expression indelibly marked on our English tongue from the origin of our language, and we find it embodied in such words as **Candlemas** and **Christmas**.

Chapter 2

The Language of the Mass

The Mass Is an Action

Many persons not familiar with the Catholic service are puzzled when assisting at Mass because the Mass is said in Latin. Now, there is no weighty reason why the Mass should be said in English, but there are many reasons why it should be said in Latin.

Why should the Mass be said in English? You will perhaps say: So that the people may understand what the priest is saying. But the Mass is not a prayer, it is an **action.** The priest is not only *praying* at the altar; he is **doing a work** which is greater than prayer. The people join with him not in the words he is saying, but in the work he is doing. This work is the offering up of sacrifice to God. What does it matter that you cannot follow the words that the priest is **saying?** You know what he is **doing**. You can, of course, if you like, get a prayerbook and follow him word for word all through the service, but this is not necessary.

The Language Is of Little Consequence

In the Old Law the people were required to be present at the sacrifices. They joined with the Hebrew priest in his great work of sacrificing. Sometimes they could not see what he was doing, much less hear anything he said. Yet they knew what he was doing, and they joined in it. When the High Priest went once a year into the Holy of Holies bearing the blood of the sacrifice, he went alone, and the people were outside, not even seeing his action, certainly not joining in any words—but knowing what his action was, and knowing that it was being done, and joining in it: each offering the victim's blood with the priest, each with his own prayers, each for his own needs.

So it is still with the Mass, the highest Act that is performed here on earth. The people who assist at the Mass all unite in the one Great Act, offering to the Most High the saving Victim. But each one offers the same in his own prayers, and for his own needs, for each man's need is different and no one carries the same cross.

The greatest act of worship ever performed was rendered on Calvary by the great High Priest. But it was done in silence. Mary, St. John and the Magdalen were present and realized what was going on. Seven times only amidst the thick darkness rang out the voice of the High Priest, and then, not always in prayer. Not all three of those who stood beneath the Cross prayed the same prayer. One was the prayer of Magdalen, who saw there before her eyes the terrible work of her own sins, and who crouched at her Lord's feet that those scarlet sins of hers might, as the blood dripped down, become white as wool. Another was the prayer of him, the innocent one, the virgin friend of the Virgin Heart, who had entered by right of his innocence into all its tenderness and understood the depths of its love. And another still was the Mother's prayer, who drew from that slow dripping blood a grander salvation than we did. She stood beneath the Cross offering the blood which she had given Him. Each with his or her own prayer, each with his or her own thoughts, as they stood beneath the Cross: but all joined in the one Sacrifice, and to all their prayers and thoughts that one great Act gave their value.

So it is today. It matters not what the language be which the priest may use at the altar; what the people join in is the great Act of worship, not a mere form of prayer, as did Mary and John and Magdalen at the feet of the Lamb bleeding His life so silently away in that Act of awful hushed worship. The externals—prayers, vestments, candles and ceremonies—are but the becoming outward dress and covering, secondary and insignificant compared with the sacred Mysteries to which they belong. They no more constitute the substance and soul of the Mass than court dress and ceremonial constitute the royal presence of the life and person of the King.

BUT WHY IN LATIN?

If there be no weighty reason for saying the Mass in English, what reasons are there for using the Latin language?

The Latin language is well adapted for the service of the Church because:

It Is a Venerable Language

It is venerable on account of its origin and its antiquity. It is the language in which the praises of God resounded from the lips of Christians during the first centuries. It is a sublime and solemn thought that the holy Sacrifice is now offered in the same language—nay, with the very same words—with which it was offered in times long past in the obscurity of the Catacombs.

It Is a Mysterious Language

Because it is a dead language, not understood by the people, there is an element of mystery about the Latin tongue. The use of an unknown tongue conveys to the mind of the people that something is going on upon the altar which is beyond their comprehension, that a mystery is being enacted. The Jews in their worship made use of the ancient Hebrew, the language of the Patriarchs. Both the Greek Catholics and the Greek schismatics employ the old form of the Greek language for divine service.

It is curious to note that the three foremost dead tongues—the Hebrew, the Greek and the Latin—were employed at the crucifixion for the inscription fixed above the thorn-crowned Head: "Jesus of Nazareth the King of the Jews." These were the languages chosen to tell the great truth to the whole world. So today, in the commemoration of the Sacrifice of the Cross, in the Mass, these three languages are still employed. The greater part of the Mass is said in Latin. The **Kyrie Eleison** is Greek. Vestiges of the Hebrew are found in the words, **Alleluia, Amen, Hosanna.**

It Fosters Unity in the Church

The use of Latin is a means of maintaining unity in the Church, as well as uniformity in her services, for the use of one and the same language in Catholic churches all over the surface of the globe is a connecting link—binding them to Rome and making one out of nations which are separated by diversity of tongues. The Universal Church must have a universal language, such as commerce has tried to make for itself in "Volapuk."*

It Safeguards Truth

A dead language is not subject to change. Languages in daily use undergo a continual process of change. Have you ever tried to read Chaucer? You will find it difficult without notes. You will meet with words that have dropped out of use and words which have changed their sense, or to which people today attach a far different meaning from the meaning which they had centuries ago. But the meaning of the words in a dead language is fixed. If a living language were employed in divine worship, heresies and errors would inevitably creep into the Church, and sacred words would be employed in an irreverent or mocking manner by the unbeliever. It must be remembered, however, that Latin is not, and never was, the only official language of the Church. The Greek, Syriac, Armenian, Coptic and Ethiopian languages are used in certain localities when celebrating the Sacred Mysteries.

* Volapuk—a language constructed in the late 19th century and intended to serve as an international language.

Chapter 3

Things Necessary for the Celebration of Mass

THE ALTAR

The greatest act of worship in the Catholic Church is the Sacrifice of the Mass. But where there is sacrifice there must also be an altar. The most prominent piece of furniture in every Catholic church is the altar. The Catholic of today can say with St. Paul: "We have an altar." (*Heb*. 13:10). We have an altar because we have a sacrifice.

The altar is usually erected in a high place elevated above the level of the floor of the church. This is done, first, that the priest may easily be seen by the faithful who assist at the Holy Sacrifice; secondly, because it represents Mount Calvary; thirdly; because it denotes the elevation of the soul from earthly things, a disposition necessary to all those who would honor God in spirit and in truth; and fourthly, because it outlines the mediation which is performed on the altar between Heaven and earth, God and man—through Christ, Who is the principal Mediator, and through the priest, who is the secondary mediator. For this reason the priest, who offers the Holy Sacrifice, is placed between Heaven and earth.

The altar represents the Table of the Lord at which Jesus sat when He instituted the Sacrifice of the Mass on the night before His bitter Passion and death. It also signifies the Cross on which Christ offered the bloody sacrifice, of which the Mass is the unbloody renewal. Above all, the altar denotes Christ, in Whom and through Whom every oblation and act of worship is offered to God. As the altar is the support of the sacrifice, from which the oblation ascends in the odor of sweetness, and without which it would return to the earth, never again to arise, so Christ is the support and strength of every sacrifice and act of worship, for nothing can be offered acceptably to God except by and through Christ.

The Altar Stone

The altar ought to be made of stone. When it is made of wood, a solid piece of natural stone, large enough to hold the Sacred Host and chalice, is inserted into or placed on the surface of the wooden altar table. This stone is called the altar stone. This stone must be consecrated by a bishop and must have deposited therein some relics of the holy martyrs.

The altar is made of stone because it denotes Christ, Who is the mystical stone, a name often applied to Him in the Sacred Scriptures. He is called the foundation stone, the corner stone, the rock of the desert: "And the rock was Christ" (*1 Cor.* 10:4)—the rock which, being struck not by the rod of Moses but by that of the Passion, pours forth most copiously the waters of divine grace. The altar is made of stone because stone is symbolic of solidity and shows how the divine worship is most firmly established on Christ.

The altar stone is anointed with oil to denote Christ, Who is anointed with divinity, anointed with the priesthood, anointed with the fullness and abundance of the Holy Spirit, Who operates unto the sanctification of all Christians.

The consecrated altar stone contains the relics of the holy martyrs. Relics are inserted into the altar stone to remind us of the ancient practice of celebrating the Sacred Mysteries over the tombs of the martyrs in the Catacombs. This custom also manifests the intimate union of Christ with the faithful in the same sacrifice. The martyrs laid down their lives in union with and by virtue of Christ's sacrifice on the Cross. It is for this reason that we find many altars made in the form of a tomb.

The Tabernacle

Originally the altar was made in the shape of an ordinary table. By degrees, behind the altar a step was introduced, raised slightly above it, for candlesticks, flowers, reliquaries and other ornaments. This step was called the altar ledge. Later, the tabernacle was added as a stationary appendix of the altar, and at its sides and behind it, other steps were placed.

The name of tabernacle, or tent, is given to the Eucharistic habitation of Our Lord from the sacred tent of the Israelites (*Ex.* 26), which served as their sanctuary before the erection of Solomon's Temple. By the tabernacle we understand the receptacle or case placed upon the table of the altar, or built into the altar, in which the vessels containing the Blessed Sacrament are kept. It occupies the center of the altar. The tabernacle is most sacred to every Catholic heart because behind its door dwells the "Prisoner of Love." "Behold the Tabernacle of God with men and He will dwell with them." (*Apoc.* 21:3).

THE ALTAR FURNISHINGS

Crucifix

The crucifix is the principal ornament of the altar. The image of the Crucified raised upon the altar indicates that the Eucharistic altar is a true Calvary, on which the bloody sacrifice of Christ is renewed in an unbloody manner. It should be large enough to be conveniently seen by both the celebrant and the people, so that it may attract the eyes and hearts of all toward it: "And I, if I be lifted up from the earth, will draw all things to myself." (*John* 12:32). The Cross is the emblem of the triumph of Our Lord, Who, in expiring upon it, conquered the world.

Candles

The candlesticks and candles crown the altar. Before the tenth century, the candles were not placed on the altar, but were held by the acolytes or placed on the floor near the altar. This is still the custom in the Eastern Church. The candles used at Mass must be made of beeswax (at least 51%). The pure wax made by bees from flowers symbolizes the pure flesh of Christ received from His Virgin Mother. The wick signifies the soul of Christ, and the flame represents His divinity. The lights on the altar at Mass represent, likewise, the hearts of the faithful, which, illumined by the light of Christ and inflamed by the fire of His love, are ever consumed for the honor of God. The lights upon the altar also recall to our minds the faith of the first Christians, who offered up the Sacred Mysteries by the glow of the candle's light in the dark catacombs.

At a High Mass, at least four candles are required, though ordinarily six candles are used. At a Low Mass, two candles are prescribed.

Altar Cloths

The altar table, usually called the *mensa,* which is the Latin word for "table," is covered with three linen cloths. These are used to absorb the Precious Blood in case of accidental spilling. The white linen marks the purity and cleanliness due to the material on which are placed the sacred gifts to be offered to Almighty God. Not only should the gift which is offered be pure, but it is important that the gift be presented in a pure manner. Accordingly, the white linen reminds us of the purity of heart with which we should always assist at the Holy Sacrifice. Linen is looked upon as an emblem of purity: "For the fine linen are the justifications of saints." (*Apoc.* 19:8). This virtue is only attained with difficulty, by vigilance and self-denial. Pure linen cloth was formerly prepared by hard and toilsome labor. The altar cloths also remind us of the winding sheets in which the body of our Saviour was wrapped before burial.

Altar Cards

To assist the memory of the priest at Mass in those prayers which he should know by heart, cards on which these prayers are printed are placed on the altar—in the center and at each end. The card on the Gospel side (the left side as one faces the altar) contains the beginning of the Gospel of St. John, which is usually recited at the end of Mass. The one on the Epistle side (the right side as one faces the altar) contains the prayer which is said by the celebrant when he blesses the cruet of water, and the psalm **Lavabo**, which is recited at the washing of the hands. The card in the center is larger than the other two because it contains more prayers.

The Missal

When the altar is prepared for the celebration of Mass, the Missal stand is placed on the Epistle side. Upon it rests the **Altar Missal** or Mass book. This book contains the prayers and Scriptural passages which are recited during the Mass. The prayers found in the Missal are most beautiful and have been gathered by the Church through the ages. The majority of these prayers have been compiled from the Holy Bible. Many of the prayers at the Mass vary from day to day in accordance with the feast that is celebrated and commemorated in the Mass. The prayers that are recited by the priest after the **Sanctus** vary seldom and very little. These prayers are called **Canon** prayers. The word **"Canon"** means **rule**, and it is used for this part of the Mass because the prayers said during it are rarely changed.

The prayers which the priest recites at the Mass are printed in black characters. The red characters or lettering which are found in the Missal are rules which guide the priest at the celebration of the Mass. These rules, printed in red characters, are called **rubrics**, from the Latin word ***ruber,*** which means **red**.

These are the most important furnishings of the altar for the celebration of the Mass. On feast days the altar is decorated with flowers, emblematic of joy and gladness.

THE ALTAR VESSELS

The Chalice

Having dealt with the altar and its furnishings, we shall next consider the altar vessels and altar linens.

The most important of the altar vessels is the **chalice**. It reminds us of the cup which our Blessed Saviour used at the Last Supper when He instituted the Holy Eucharist. That cup is known in legendary lore as the "Holy Grail" and has been immortalized by Tennyson in *The Idylls of the King* and by Richard Wagner in his famous opera *Parsifal.* The chalice is the most sacred of the altar vessels because after the Consecration it contains the Most Precious Blood of Our Lord. Since the chalice comes in contact with the Blood of Christ, it should be of the finest material. Usually the chalice is made of gold or silver; it must at least be gold-plated within. The chalice must be consecrated with holy oil by a bishop before it can be used at the Holy Sacrifice.

The Paten

To the chalice belongs the **paten**. The Eucharistic vessel known as the paten is a small shallow plate or disc of precious metal upon which the bread is offered to God at the Offertory of the Mass, and upon which the consecrated Host is again placed after the breaking. The word **paten** comes from the Latin word *patena,* used to denote a flat open vessel of the nature of a plate or dish. These vessels were used in the first centuries of the Church to collect the offerings of bread made by the faithful and also to distribute the consecrated Fragments which, after the consecrated Loaf had been broken by the celebrant, were brought down to the communicants, who in their own hands received each a portion from the patena. Toward the end of the ninth century, when the zeal of the faithful regarding the frequent reception of Holy Communion declined, the system of consecrating the bread offered by the faithful and of distributing Communion from the patena seems gradually to have changed, and the large paten was no longer used. It was probably about this time that the custom originated for the priest himself to use a paten at the altar to hold the sacred Host and thus do away with the danger of scattering the Particles after the breaking of the consecrated Host.

The paten, like the chalice, must be made of precious material, and it cannot be used before it has been consecrated with chrism by a bishop. These sacred vessels should be made of precious material and must be consecrated by special prayers and unctions (anointings) on account of the great respect that is due the sacred Body and Blood of Our Lord.

The Ciborium

The **ciborium** is that sacred vessel in which the small hosts, altar breads, are consecrated for the Communion of the people. In it the consecrated Hosts are reserved. The name is derived from the Latin word ***cibus,*** "food," because the ciborium is used to contain the Heavenly Bread. In shape the ciborium resembles a chalice, but the cup or bowl is round rather than oblong and is provided with a conical cover surmounted by a cross. When the ciborium contains the sacred species, it should be covered with a white silken veil.

During the first three centuries, the Blessed Eucharist was not generally reserved in churches, owing to the danger of profanation and to the persecutions. The faithful sometimes kept the sacred species* in silver boxes in their homes for the purpose of receiving Holy Communion at the time of death. This information is gleaned from the writings of St. Jerome and Tertullian. When the persecutions subsided, the practice of reserving the Blessed Eucharist in the churches became general. The vessel in which the sacred species were kept was commonly called the ciborium. The ciborium was kept either in a chamber in the sacristy or in a niche in the wall or in a pillar. Today the ciborium with the sacred species is preserved in the tabernacle.

The Ostensorium (or Monstrance)

In speaking of the altar vessels, mention must be made of the **ostensorium** or **monstrance** and **lunula**, although these sacred vessels are not used at the Sacrifice of the Mass. The ostensorium is a vessel or shrine used to expose the Blessed Sacrament for the adoration of the faithful. It is called "ostensorium" from the Latin word *ostendere,* which means to "show." It usually has the form of the sun emitting its rays to all sides. In the middle of the ostensorium there is a receptacle of such a size that a large Host may easily be put into it.

The **lunula** is a little case of gold or of silver, having a double glass, in which the Sacred Host is enclosed in order to place it in the ostensorium without dan-

* *Species,* or *sacred species:* the two forms—the form of bread and the form of wine—under which the Body and Blood of Christ are present after the Consecration.

ger of breaking the Host. It is called ***lunula,*** which is the Latin word for "little moon," because it usually has the form of a crescent.*

Some worldlings are inclined to ask, as Judas did when Magdalen anointed Our Lord's feet: "To what purpose is this waste?" when they see the care and money expended by Catholics on the sacred vessels. They should, however, consider how greatly the beauty of God's house impresses the beholder and conduces to devotion. It is only right and just to give what is most precious and beautiful for the service of God.

THE ALTAR LINENS

Why Linen Is Prescribed

The sacred linens used at the Sacrifice of the Mass are the corporal, the pall and the purificator. It is strictly prescribed that linen only shall be used about the altar. This is in accordance with an old custom that owes its origin to the fact that the dead body of Christ was wrapped in linen before it was laid in the sepulchre. Moreover, linen is emblematic of sincerity and purity of heart: "for the fine linen are the justifications of saints." (*Apoc.* 19:18).

Because these linens come in contact with the sacred species during the Sacrifice of the Mass, the laity are not permitted to touch them after they have been used for the Holy Sacrifice. A priest, or a person who has permission from the Bishop, washes these linens in three different waters, which are afterwards poured into the sacrarium (a special sink which drains into

* When brought to the sick, the Sacred Host is carried in a small gold case called a pyx (pronunciation: pix).

the earth, not the sewer). It is only after they have been washed in this manner that these linens are given to a lay person to be laundered or mended.

The Corporal

The corporal is a square linen napkin about fifteen by fifteen inches. The name **corporal** comes from the Latin word ***corpus,*** which means **"body."** This name is given to this linen napkin because the Body of Christ, under the appearance of bread, rests upon it during the Holy Sacrifice. The edges of the corporal are sometimes ornamented with fine lace, and a red cross is embroidered in it near the edge. At the beginning of the Mass it is spread out at full length in the center of the altar, over the altar cloths. It must be large enough to hold the chalice, the large hosts (altar breads), and also the ciborium containing the smaller hosts for the Communion of the laity. Originally it was longer and wider than the one in use at present. It covered the whole table of the altar and was looked upon as a fourth altar cloth. For reasons of convenience and reverence, the folded corporal is carried to and from the altar in a square, pocket-shaped receptacle which is called a **burse.** When the chalice is carried to and from the altar, the burse is placed on the chalice, over the veil. Like the veil of the chalice, the burse is of the same material and color as the vestments with which it is used.

The Pall

Originally the pall was not distinct from the corporal, because the latter was so large as to do away with the need of a distinct pall, and the posterior part of the corporal was so arranged that it could easily be drawn over the host and chalice. When the corporal was reduced to its present size, the pall became a distinct cover of the chalice.

The name **pall** is derived from the Latin word ***pallium,*** meaning **"coverlet."** The **pall**, as used at the Mass, is a linen coverlet about six inches square. It may be a large piece of linen, or it may consist of two pieces of linen between which a piece of cardboard is inserted for the sake of stiffening it. The upper side is usually ornamented. It is used to prevent anything from falling into the chalice. It should be large enough to cover the paten. Like the corporal, it must be blessed before it may be used at Mass.

The Purificator

The purificator is a piece of pure white linen which the priest uses to wipe the chalice, as well as his lips and fingers at the ablutions after Communion. It is called **purificator** because it is used to cleanse or purify the chalice. It is usually twelve or eighteen inches long and nine or ten inches wide. It is folded in three layers so that when placed on the chalice, beneath the paten, its width is about three inches.

From the great care which the Church takes to surround the Sacred Mysteries with all that is pure and clean, we are reminded of the purity and sanctity that must ever adorn the soul that would draw near its God present under the sacramental species. It was He Who said: "Blessed are the clean of heart."

Chapter 4

The Eucharistic Elements

The Altar Bread (Host)

There are two Eucharistic elements, bread and wine. The bread used as the matter of the Holy Sacrifice must be made from wheaten flour. The bread required for the Mass is that formed of wheaten flour, and no other kind of flour is allowed for the altar bread, such as, for example, that which is ground from rye, barley or corn. The reason why the Church prescribes wheaten bread is that the Bible tells us that at the Last Supper, "Jesus took bread . . ." In Scripture, the word **bread** without any qualifying addition always signifies wheaten bread. When eating the Pasch, the Jews used only wheaten bread. No doubt Christ adhered to this Jewish custom of using only wheaten bread in the Passover Supper and, by the words "**Do this** for a commemoration of me," commanded its use for all succeeding times.

The bread used at the Mass must be unleavened. By *leavened* bread is meant such wheaten bread as requires leaven or yeast in its preparation or baking. Unleavened bread (*azyma*) is formed from a mixture of wheaten flour and water which has been kneaded into dough and then baked. The Church prescribes the use of unleavened bread because the Scriptures inform us that the Last Supper was celebrated "on the first day of the azymes." (The Greek Church, however, uses leavened bread for the Eucharist.) The unleavened bread indicates the purity of soul which all should acquire and which is obtained only through Christ. Leaven denotes vice and the principle of all corruption. "Know ye not that a little leaven corrupteth the whole mass? Purge out the old leaven, that you may be a new paste, as you are unleavened." (*1 Cor.* 5:6-7).

The altar bread is of a circular form. Pictures in the catacombs show that the early Christians used round altar breads. The circle is the most perfect of figures and is symbolic of eternity and infinity. On this account it is the most appropriate figure to represent the presence of Him Who is without beginning and without end. (*Heb.* 7:3). The altar bread or host which the priest uses at Mass is larger than the hosts which are used when Communion is given to the people. It should be of such a size that it may be seen by the people when held up to their gaze at the Elevation. The altar bread is placed on the paten when the chalice is prepared in the sacristy.

In the first centuries of the Church, the bread and wine to be used at the Eucharistic Sacrifice were brought by the faithful. These offerings of bread and wine were collected before the Offertory, and as much as was necessary for the Communion of the celebrant and the faithful was consecrated.

The Altar Wine

The second Eucharistic element required for the Holy Sacrifice is wine of the grape. Wine of the grape is prescribed by the Church on account of the example and the command of Christ, Who at the Last Supper certainly converted the natural wine of grapes into His Blood. The rite of the Jewish Passover required the head of the family to pass around the "cup of benediction" containing the wine of grapes. Moreover, at the Last Supper Christ expressly declared that henceforth He would not drink of the "fruit of the vine . . ." (*Luke* 22:18). Because at the first Consecration which was performed in this world the elements of bread and wine were chosen to represent the immolation of Christ's body and blood, the Church has ever been faithful to the command of the Master, "Do this in commemoration of Me." The wine which is to be used at Mass is put into a small glass cruet which is placed on a table on the Epistle side of the altar.

Why Bread and Wine?

Christ might have chosen some other elements to represent His bloody sacrifice. But He desired bread and wine to be the matter of the sacrifice because bread and wine are found everywhere. Bread and wine constitute man's most natural and strengthening sustenance. Therefore the Psalmist sings of the Lord's blessing of the earth, "that bread may strengthen man's heart," and "that wine may cheer the heart of man." (*Ps*. 103).

The use of bread and wine also discloses to us a number of the mysteries of Faith. Bread and wine, which form the food of man, signify in the first place that Christ Our Lord is the healthful nutriment of our souls. They signify in the second place the union of the faithful among themselves and with Christ; for as the bread is made from numerous grains, and the wine from many grapes, so the one mystical Body of Christ is formed from the multitude of the faithful. They remind us in the third place of the mortification which everyone must endure in order to be united with Christ. For just as wheat must be ground in the mill in order to be made into bread, and the grapes must be pressed, in like manner a faithful soul must die to himself in order to be intimately united with Christ and live with His spirit.

The Church elevates and sanctifies nature by using sensible objects in her worship. She consecrates and deifies the wheat and the grape. They become the means of the highest act of worship.

"Sweet Jesus, all on earth I see
Live, bloom, and labor but for Thee;
The golden wheat grows, and the vine
To form the soul's sweet food divine."

Why should the wheat and the grape grow when the Holy Sacrifice has ceased? Why should the olive grow when it can no longer be the food that feeds the flame of love before the tabernacle? Why should the tree give its incense when the fire of the sanctuary is extinguished? Why should the virgin bee form its waxen cell when the taper no longer burns on the altar? Why should the flowers grow and shed their perfume when Jesus' presence is forgotten? Why should the earth exist when Jesus dwells there no longer in His Sacrament of love?

Chapter 5

Vestments Used at Mass

Why Special Vestments Are Prescribed

The Mass, inasmuch as it is a lively representation of Christ's sacrifice on Calvary, may be considered as a drama, whose theater is the altar, whose actor is the priest representing the person of Christ, and whose action is performed in a series of ceremonies.

When enacting the great drama at the altar the priest wears certain robes prescribed by the Church. The use of special dress for public functionaries is in accord with the very nature of man and is common among the most savage as well as the most civilized nations. God Himself gave directions concerning the vestments which were to be worn by the priests under the Old Testament. (*Ex.* 28:4). In the Christian dispensation, the Church has done the same.

By prescribing certain vestments for the priest at the altar, the Church wishes to remind us that the priest does not act at the altar in his own person. He acts as the representative of Christ. When an official appears publicly in the name of his sovereign, he wears a distinctive uniform. Now, the priest goes to the altar in the service and in the name of the Supreme Lord: therefore, it is becoming that he should appear robed in a becoming manner. Moreover, it would seem unbecoming for the priest to perform the most sacred of functions in his usual attire.

Origin of Vestments

The vestments, then, which the priest uses at Mass were not prescribed by Christ, but by the Church in the course of time. In the early centuries of the Church the dress of daily life was worn at the services of the Church. Under normal conditions, better garments were used at the sacred functions. The Christian vestments were not patterned after the priestly dress of the Old Testament. They have, rather, developed from the secular dress of the Graeco-Roman world. During the course of centuries the Church vestments underwent many changes.

Before robing himself in the sacerdotal vestments, the priest, clad in his cassock, washes his hands. It has been the custom of all times and of all nations for the ministers of the altar to wash their hands previous to offering sacrifice. The Old Testament expressly commanded this observance. (*Ex.* 30:18). This act reminds the priest of the purity that should adorn his soul when ministering before the Most High. While performing this ceremony in the sacristy, the priest prays: "Grant to my hands, O Lord, a virtue that shall cleanse away every stain, so that I may be able to serve Thee with a clean mind and body."

The Amice

The priest then proceeds with the vesting. He first puts on the **amice**, a linen cloth which is placed around the neck, with folds falling upon the shoulders. This vestment is called **amice** from the Latin word ***amicire,*** meaning **"to wrap around."** The amice was introduced to hide the bare throat and to protect the other vestments from being soiled by perspiration.

The amice represents the cloth with which the soldiers blindfolded Our Lord when they struck Him. When the priest puts on the amice, he prays: "Place upon my head, O Lord, the helmet of salvation to resist the assaults of the enemy."

The Alb

The **alb** comes next. It is a white linen garment, with close fitting sleeves, reaching nearly to the ground and secured around the waist by a cord. The name **alb** is also derived from the Latin, namely from ***albus,*** which means **"white."** A white linen tunic was a common feature of secular attire with the Romans, especially on festive occasions. This white garment symbolizes the chastity befitting a priest. It reminds us also of the white robe in which Herod arrayed Our Lord in mockery. The priest recites this prayer when putting on the alb: "Purify me, O Lord, from all stain and cleanse my heart, that washed in the blood of the Lamb, I may enjoy eternal delights."

The Cincture

The **cincture** is a cord used to confine the loose-flowing alb and prevent it from impeding the movements of the wearer. This word is derived from the Latin word ***cingere,*** meaning **"to gird."** The use of the cincture recalls to mind the cords which were tied around the sacred body of Our Lord. It denotes, moreover, the mortification of the flesh and its vices. Wherefore the priest prays thus: "Gird me, O Lord, with the cincture of purity and extinguish in my loins the heat of concupiscence, that the virtue of continence and chastity may abide in me."

The Maniple

The **maniple** is an ornamental vestment in the form of a band, about a yard long and four inches wide. It is worn on the left arm in such a manner that it falls in equal lengths on both sides of the arm. The maniple is made of silk. It is worn only during Mass. For the sub-deacon, the maniple is the liturgical sign of his rank. Originally the maniple was an ornamental handkerchief, which was seldom put into actual use but was generally carried in the hand as an ornament. Ornamental handkerchiefs or cloths of this kind were carried by people of rank in ordinary life. The **mappa** with which the consul or praetor gave the signal for the commencement of the games was a similar cloth.

The Latin word ***manipulus*** means a **"small bundle"** or **"handful."** The name was given to this cloth because it was folded together and carried in the left hand. The maniple reminds us of the chains with which Our Lord was bound during His Passion. As the word **maniple** means **sheaf** or **bundle**, it also reminds the priest that he must not appear empty-handed in the presence of God but that he must bear the fruits of virtue and good works. Putting on the maniple, the priest prays: "May I deserve, O Lord, to bear the maniple of weeping and sorrow, that with exultation I may receive the reward of my labor." The Psalmist says: "Going they went and wept, casting their seeds. But coming they shall come with joyfulness, carrying their sheaves." (*Ps.* 125:6-7).

The Stole

The **stole** is a liturgical vestment in the form of a long band which is placed over the shoulders and crossed upon the breast. It is made of silk and richly ornamented. The stole was formerly a white linen garment. The name is derived from the Latin ***stola,*** which was the distinctive garment of the nobility. It was decorated in front with a magnificent border. This border alone the Church preserves and gives to it the name **stole**.

The stole signifies the yoke of the Lord, consisting of the burdens of the sacred ministry. At the ordination service the bishop imposes the stole upon the candidate for the priesthood and says: "Take upon you the yoke of the Lord, for His yoke is sweet and His burden light." The stole also signifies the nuptial garment of grace. When putting on the stole, the priest prays: "Restore to me, O Lord, the stole of immortality which I lost through the transgression of my first parents, and though I approach unworthily to celebrate Thy Sacred Mystery, may I merit nevertheless eternal joy."

The Chasuble

The **chasuble** is the last and the most richly adorned of the sacred vestments. It is worn above all the rest. It must be remembered that the Mass vestments are adaptations of the secular attire commonly worn throughout the Roman Empire in the early Christian centuries. The priest, discharging his sacred functions at the altar, was dressed as in civil life. The custom gradually grew up of reserving for this purpose garments that were newer and cleaner than those used in his daily avocations.

The chasuble in particular seems to have been identical with the ordinary outer garment of the lower orders. It consisted of a square or circular piece of cloth, in the center of which a hole was made. Through this the head was passed. With the arms hanging down, this garment covered the whole figure. It was like a little house. The Latin word for **"little house"** is ***casula.*** From this we derive the word **chasuble**. One can readily see that the primitive chasuble was very inconvenient for the priest. It was impossible to use arms or hands without lifting the whole of the front part of the vestment. To remedy this, the sides were gradually cut away until the vestment received its present form. That part of the chasuble which covers the priest's back has a large cross embroidered upon it.

The chasuble reminds us of the purple garment which Christ wore in the courtroom of Pilate. The cross embroidered upon the chasuble recalls to mind the Cross which Christ carried to Calvary. When the bishop vests the newly ordained priest with the chasuble, he says: "Receive this sacerdotal garment by which charity is denoted." When the priest puts on the chasuble before the Mass, he prays: "O Lord, Who hast said: My yoke is sweet and My burden light, grant that I may so carry it as to merit Thy grace."

Color of the Vestments

The inner vestments of the priest are always white and are intended to represent the interior purity and innocence of heart which should never be put aside, but which should be preserved under the cloak of charity.

The chasuble, or outer garment, admits of a variety of colors. The chasuble signifies charity, which is the root and parent from which the other virtues spring. Moreover, charity in itself embraces and manifests all kinds of virtues, even as the resplendent light of the sun diffuses many rays of all colors.

The Church uses in her liturgy five different colors: white, red, green, violet and black. **White** signifies innocence and spiritual joy, and is used on feasts of Our Lord and of such saints as were not martyrs. **Red** denotes not only the fire of charity, which the Holy Spirit enkindles and diffuses in us, but likewise the blood of the martyrs, the most excellent flower of charity. It is used at Whitsuntide (the season of Pentecost) and on the feasts of martyrs. **Green** is symbolic of hope and of the Christian's yearning for Heaven. It is used on Sundays after Epiphany and Pentecost. **Violet** signifies humility and penance and is therefore used during Lent and Advent. **Black** is the color of sorrow and mourning and is used on Good Friday and at Masses for the dead (Requiem Masses). Rose-colored vestments may be used at Mass on the Third Sunday of Advent, which is known as "Gaudete Sunday," and on the fourth Sunday of Lent, which is known as "Laetare Sunday." These are days of restrained rejoicing. The rose color is emblematic of joy mingled with sorrow, for every rose has its thorn. Vestments made of gold cloth may be used instead of the white, red or green vestments.

As the face of nature changes with the varying seasons, so the different emotions evoked by the various seasons of the ecclesiastical year find expression in the use of different colors.

Chapter 6

A Word on Ceremonies

A **ceremony** (from the Latin ***caerimonia***) is an act prescribed by law. In the Liturgy, an external action, gesture or movement which accompanies the prayers and public exercise of divine worship is called a ceremony.

Ceremony is the necessary outcome of man's spiritual and material nature. Hence man must pay God a twofold adoration: one spiritual, which consists in the interior devotion of the soul; the other material, which manifests itself in the outward form of worship. There is no inward sentiment or feeling which man is not accustomed to express outwardly by some suitable gesture or action.

Ceremonies are employed to embellish and adorn sacred functions, to excite in the faithful sentiments of respect and devotion, to impart a knowledge of the mysteries of religion and to elevate our minds by these external things to the contemplation of divine things.

Ceremonies are founded on Holy Scripture. Christ hardly ever performed a miracle without using some ceremony: as when He blessed bread and fishes (*Matt.* 15:36); when He spread clay upon the eyes of a blind man (*John* 9:6); when He prayed on bended knees (*Luke* 22:41); when He breathed upon His disciples (*John* 20:22); and finally, when He blessed them with uplifted hands before ascending into Heaven. (*Luke* 24:50).

The ceremonies of the Mass were instituted by the Church not only "to display the majesty of this august Sacrifice, but also to excite the minds of the faithful, through these signs of religion and piety, to the contemplation of the profound mysteries which are concealed in the Eucharistic Sacrifice." (Council of Trent, Session XXII, Chap. V).

The purpose, therefore, of the Church in using ceremonies is twofold: the first is to manifest the respect and reverence due to the divine Sacrifice; and the second is to point out by these signs the profound mysteries which lie concealed therein.

Chapter 7

Rules of Posture for Assisting at Mass

These rules indicate the attitude or posture which the Church desires as most suitable to the various parts of the Mass. They do not bind so strictly as to make it a sin to depart from them. The same customs do not prevail in all places; therefore, one should always conform to the local custom.

Low Mass

STAND	Priest enters Sanctuary
KNEEL	PRAYERS AT FOOT OF ALTAR
KNEEL	INTROIT
KNEEL	GLORIA
KNEEL	EPISTLE
STAND	GOSPEL
STAND	CREED (Kneel on the right knee at *"et incarnatus est . . . ET HOMO FACTUS EST."*)
SIT	OFFERTORY (after priest says *"Oremus"*)
KNEEL	SANCTUS
STAND	LAST GOSPEL (Kneel on the right knee at *"ET VERBUM CARO FACTUM EST."*)
KNEEL	PRAYERS AFTER LOW MASS
STAND	Until priest leaves Sanctuary

High Mass

STAND	Priest enters Sanctuary
KNEEL	PRAYERS AT FOOT OF ALTAR
KNEEL	INTROIT
STAND	GLORIA
SIT	When priest sits down while Gloria is being sung.
STAND	When priest stands to return to altar. Remain standing until Epistle.
SIT	EPISTLE
STAND	GOSPEL
STAND	CREED
SIT	When priest sits down while Creed is being sung. (Kneel on both knees when the choir sings *"et incarnatus est . . . ET HOMO FACTUS EST."*)
STAND	*When priest stands to return to altar.*
SIT	OFFERTORY (after priest says *"Oremus"*)
STAND	*"PER OMNIA SAECULA SAECULORUM"* (at end of Secret) through PREFACE
KNEEL	SANCTUS
STAND	*"PER OMNIA SAECULA SAECULORUM"* through PATER NOSTER
KNEEL	At end of PATER NOSTER *(". . . Et ne nos inducas in tentationem. Amen.")*
STAND	POSTCOMMUNION *(Priest says "Oremus")*
KNEEL	LAST BLESSING
STAND	LAST GOSPEL (Kneel on one knee at *"ET VERBUM CARO FACTUM EST."*)
STAND	Until priest leaves Sanctuary

Chapter 8

The Asperges

The priest sprinkles the congregation with Holy Water.

The choir sings the following anthems while the priest sprinkles the congregation:

Thou shalt sprinkle me with hyssop, O Lord, and I shall be cleansed: Thou shalt wash me, and I shall be made whiter than snow.

Have mercy on me, O God, according to Thy great mercy.

Glory be to the Father and to the Son and to the Holy Ghost. As it was in the beginning, is now, and ever shall be, world without end. Amen.

Thou shalt sprinkle me, etc.

Returning to the altar, the priest says:

Priest: Show us, O Lord, Thy mercy.

Choir: And grant us Thy salvation.

Priest: O Lord, hear my prayer.

Choir: And let my cry come unto Thee.

Priest: The Lord be with you.

Choir: And with thy spirit.

Priest: Let us pray: Graciously hear us, O holy Lord, Father Almighty, Eternal God; and be pleased to send Thy holy angel from Heaven, to guard, cherish, protect, visit and defend all who dwell in this house. Through Christ our Lord.

Choir: Amen.

A function peculiar to the Catholic Sunday service is the **Asperges**. The **Asperges** takes place before the High Mass, the principal service of the Church on Sunday. Non-Catholics often look on in surprise when witnessing this function, asking themselves what significance this peculiar ceremony might have.

By the **Asperges** we mean the rite of sprinkling the congregation with holy water. The function is called **Asperges** from the words intoned at the beginning of the ceremony. "Asperges" is a Latin word derived from the word ***aspergere,*** which means to **"wash,"** or to **"sprinkle."**

The ceremony is performed by the celebrant, the priest who is about to celebrate the Mass. He enters the sanctuary wearing vestments of the liturgical color of the day. In place of the **chasuble** he wears the **cope.** Having made a genuflection before the altar, he kneels down and, with the aspersorial, sprinkles the altar, himself and the servers with holy water, intoning the while the first words of the ninth verse of Psalm 50, ***"Asperges me"*****—"Thou shalt sprinkle me**." Making a genuflection before the altar, the celebrant sprinkles the congregation, usually walking down and back up through the main aisle of the church, though he need not go beyond the gate of the sanctuary.

After the priest has intoned ***"Asperges me"*****—"Thou shalt sprinkle me,"** and while he is sprinkling the congregation, the choir continues the anthem, singing: **"with hyssop, O Lord, and I shall be cleansed: Thou shalt wash me, and I shall be made whiter than snow."** Then the first verse of the 50th Psalm is chanted: **"Have mercy on me, O God, according to Thy great mercy."** To this the minor doxology is added: **"Glory be to the Father,"** etc. After the doxology, the ninth verse of the Psalm is repeated.

The use of these words of the 50th Psalm is most appropriate. The people are about to assist at the great Sacrifice of the New Law. They realize that a soul steeped in sin is an abomination in the sight of God. Hence, mindful of their many sins, they cry out to God for mercy as David did after he had sinned with Bethsabee. It is the "Miserere" of the soul conscious of its sin and longing to be reconciled with its Maker.

The words of the text are clear, with the exception of the word "hyssop." Hyssop is an aromatic plant. It is referred to in several passages of Holy Scripture. In *Exodus* 12:22, Moses is represented as bidding the elders of Israel to take a bunch of hyssop and to sprinkle with it the blood of the paschal lamb upon the lintel and the side posts of the doors of their dwellings. In *Exodus* 24:8, another reference is made to hyssop. According to this passage, Israel's great lawgiver sprinkled the Hebrews with hyssop dipped in the blood of victims at the sealing of the old covenant between Yahweh and His people. Hyssop was also used at some of the purifications of the Jews. With it the sprinkling of the water of purification was made at the cleansing of a person polluted by the touch of a dead body. (*Num.* 19:8). It is therefore not surprising to find that this intimate Law led the Psalmist to regard the sprinkling with hyssop as symbolical of a thorough purification of the heart. And this view the Catholic Church has made her own in the ceremony of the **Asperges**. When, therefore, in the language of the Psalmist we ask in the **Asperges** that God sprinkle us with hyssop, we ask Him to cleanse our souls from sin so that we may assist worthily at the Sacrifice of the Mass.

Ordinarily water is used for cleansing purposes. By

using it at this function, the Church wishes to remind the faithful who are about to assist at Mass that they should first cleanse their souls from sin through sincere repentance. The water which is used for this ceremony is first blessed, hence we call it Holy Water. "Every creature," says St. Paul, "is sanctified by the word of God and prayer." (*1 Tim*. 4:4-5). When the Church blesses water, she asks Almighty God to protect and bless all those who use it with reverence and devotion.

The Vidi Aquam

From Easter to Pentecost inclusive, instead of the **Asperges** the **Vidi Aquam** is sung: **"I saw water coming forth from the Temple on the right side, Alleluia. And all those to whom this water came were saved, and they shall say: Alleluia, alleluia."** This is followed by a verse from the 117th Psalm: **"Give praise to the Lord, for He is good: for His mercy endureth for ever."** The other prayers and responses are the same as on other Sundays. The words of the anthem ***"Vidi Aquam"*—"I saw water,"** etc.—are taken from the 47th chapter of *Ezechiel*. These waters of which the prophet speaks are not to be understood literally but mystically, of the waters of Baptism or of the water which flowed from the side of Christ, through the merits of Whose Passion all may be saved. It is appropriate to sing of these redeeming virtues of the waters of Baptism or of the Passion of Christ during Eastertide, or Paschal Time,* because at this time the Church celebrates the triumph of the Redeemer.

---

* Paschal Time or Eastertide, the Easter Season, runs liturgically from Easter Sunday (actually, from the Easter Vigil service on Holy Saturday) through Trinity Sunday.

PART THREE

The Prayers and Ceremonies of the Mass

Pronunciation of Three Latin Phrases Used Repeatedly in the Latin Mass

Oremus. (oh-**ray**-moos)	**Let us pray.**
Dominus vobiscum. (**Doe**-mee-nus voe-**bees**-kum)	**The Lord be with you.**
Et cum spiritu tuo. (Et koom **speer**-ee-too **too**-oh)	**And with thy spirit.**

Chapter 1

The Preparatory Part of the Mass

"The Mass of the Catechumens"

The part of the Mass beginning with the Prayers at the Foot of the Altar until the Offertory may be called the "Preparatory Part of the Mass." This preparatory part consists primarily of 1) the Confiteor (Confession) at the foot of the altar; 2) the Introit; 3) the Kyrie; 4) the Gloria; 5) the Collect; 6) the Epistle; 7) the Gospel; 8) the Creed. This part of the Mass is sometimes also called "the Mass of the Catechumens." In the first ages of Christianity, persons desiring to become Christians and receive Baptism were obliged to undergo a course of instructions. They were called ***catechumens,*** a Greek word meaning persons "who are being instructed." These persons, who were not fully initiated in the teachings and practices of Christianity, were dismissed from the service before the Offertory.

The Procession to the Altar

The priest, accompanied by his attendants, proceeds from the sacristy to the altar.

Vested in his sacred vestments, accompanied by the

acolytes or servers, the priest proceeds to the altar. In his left hand he carries the chalice covered with a veil. His right hand rests upon the burse which covers the top of the chalice. Arriving at the foot of the altar, the priest bares his head by removing the biretta, which he hands to one of the acolytes. The biretta, emblematic of the priest's dignity and power, replaces the amice which in olden times served as a covering for the celebrant's head. If the Holy Eucharist is reserved in the tabernacle of the altar upon which the Holy Sacrifice is to take place, the priest genuflects, or bends his knee, before the altar. The genuflection is an external act of adoration paid to the Divine Majesty. As the genuflection is an act of adoration, we do not bend our knee before the images of the Saints, because we adore God alone. The genuflection is also an act expressive of that humility which every man must feel in the presence of the Most High.

Having adored his God, the priest ascends the altar steps and goes to the altar. The chalice is deposited upon the altar a little to the left. The burse is removed from the top of the chalice, and having taken the corporal therefrom, the priest places it against the altar ledge to his left. The corporal is then spread out in the center of the altar, and the chalice, still veiled, is placed upon it. Having arranged the chalice, the celebrant walks to the Epistle side of the altar, opens the Missal and arranges the markers so that the prayers proper to the day's feast may easily be found. It must be remembered that many of the prayers recited at the Mass vary from day to day in accordance with the feast or mystery that is being celebrated.* Having

* These variable prayers and Scripture readings are referred to collectively as the **Proper** of the Mass; the prayers which remain

adjusted the markers in the Missal, the priest again goes to the center of the altar, bows his head before the altar crucifix and descends to the foot of the altar.

PRAYERS AT THE FOOT OF THE ALTAR**

The priest prays at the foot of the altar.

P. In the name of the Father, ✠ and of the Son, and of the Holy Ghost. Amen.

P. I will go unto the altar of God.
S. To God, Who giveth joy to my youth.

The "Judica Me" (Psalm 42)

P. Judge me, O God, and defend my cause against the ungodly nation; deliver me from the unjust and deceitful man.
S. For Thou, O God, art my strength, why hast Thou cast me off? And why do I go sorrowful, while the enemy afflicts me?
P. Send forth Thy light and Thy truth; they have conducted me and brought me unto Thy holy mount, and unto Thy tabernacles.
S. Then I will go unto the altar of God, to God, Who giveth joy to my youth.

---

the same in every Mass are referred to collectively as the **Ordinary** of the Mass.

** The wording of the Mass prayers in English may vary from missal to missal. The official texts are the *Latin* texts; the Latin is the same from missal to missal, but there is no official English translation of the Latin text of the Traditional Latin Mass.

P. I will praise Thee on the harp, O God, my God. Why art thou sorrowful, O my soul, and why dost thou disquiet me?

S. Hope in God, for I will still praise Him, the salvation of my countenance and my God.

P. Glory be to the Father, and to the Son, and to the Holy Ghost.

S. As it was in the beginning, is now, and ever shall be, world without end. Amen.

P. I will go unto the altar of God.

S. To God, Who giveth joy to my youth.

(Begin here at Mass for the dead and in Passiontide:)

P. Our help is in the name of the Lord.

S. Who made heaven and earth.

The Confiteor

P. I confess to Almighty God, to blessed Mary ever Virgin, to blessed Michael the Archangel, to blessed John the Baptist, to the holy Apostles Peter and Paul, to all the Saints, and to you, brethren, that I have sinned exceedingly in thought, word and deed, (*strike breast three times:*) through my fault, through my fault, through my most grievous fault. Therefore I beseech blessed Mary ever Virgin, blessed Michael the Archangel, blessed John the Baptist, the holy Apostles Peter and Paul, and all the Saints, and to you, brethren, to pray to the Lord our God for me.

S. May Almighty God have mercy upon you, forgive you your sins and bring you to everlasting life.

Note: **P.** stands for Priest, **S.** stands for Server(s). A small cross within the text of a Mass prayer indicates that the priest makes a Sign of the Cross at that point.

P. Amen.
S. I confess to Almighty God, etc.

(The server repeats the Confiteor, substituting the word "father" for "brethren.")

P. May Almighty God have mercy upon you, forgive you your sins and bring you to everlasting life.
S. Amen.
P. May the Almighty ✠ and merciful Lord grant us pardon, absolution and remission of our sins.
S. Amen.
P. O God, Thou wilt turn again and quicken us.
S. And Thy people shall rejoice in Thee.
P. Show us, O Lord, Thy mercy.
S. And grant us Thy salvation.
P. O Lord, hear my prayer.
S. And let my cry come unto Thee.
P. The Lord be with you.
S. And with thy spirit.

Everything is now set for the great drama. Arrived at the foot of the altar, the priest stands, as it were, on the threshold of the Most High. What thoughts flood his mind at this solemn moment! With Jacob he may say: "How terrible is this place! This is no other but the house of God, and the gate of heaven." (*Gen*. 28:17). From within he seems to hear a voice that says: Halt, "for the place whereon thou standest is holy ground." (*Ex*. 3:5). Overcome by awe he humbly bends his knee in adoration. But God demands sacrifice. The people, too, demand that this highest form of worship be paid to the Most High. Hence the priest arises, signs himself with the Sign of the Cross and begins the great act. **"In the name of the Father and of the Son and of the Holy Ghost. Amen."**

Knowing that the highest form of worship that can be rendered to God is sacrifice, and grasping the significance of the Master's words, "Do this in commemoration of Me," the priest, unworthy though he be, now resolves to begin. He says: **"I will go unto the altar of God."** To this the acolyte, in the name of all the faithful, responds: **"To God, Who giveth joy to my youth."** (*Ps.* 42:4). It should be remembered that the acolytes or servers today perform the duties which in olden times were performed by men who had received Minor Orders. The server acts and responds in the name of the faithful. To serve Mass is the nearest approach that one who is not a priest can make to celebrating it.

The "Judica Me" (Psalm 42)

The priest who is about to celebrate the divine mysteries, awed by the Majesty of God and the sublimity of the act to be performed, stands at the foot of the altar and there, by humble prayer and the confession of sin, in union with the people whom the server represents, prepares to ascend to the altar of God.

Having made the Sign of the Cross, he recites alternately with the server the psalm of David beginning with the words, **"Judge me, O God."** (*Ps.* 42). This psalm was composed by David when he was persecuted by Saul and kept at a distance from the Temple of God. It expresses his ardent desire of approaching the Tabernacle to offer prayer and sacrifice to God. The principal reason for introducing this psalm is found in the verse, **"I will go unto the altar of God, to God Who giveth joy to my youth."**

David, and the Church after his example, asks in this psalm to be freed from the attacks of the enemy, that is, from sin and temptation, that he may piously offer the Sacrifice to the praise of the Divine Majesty. In the spiritual sense, this psalm applies to the just man, who in the trials of the present life longs to leave this world and to go to his heavenly country. A paraphrase of this psalm might be made to read:

1. O God, have regard for the cause of my soul against my spiritual enemies, and deliver me from all defilement.
2. O God, Thou art not so much my Judge as Thou art my strength and help. Why, then, should I be sorrowful, as one deprived of Thy favor and overcome by his enemies?
3. Send forth, I beseech Thee, the light of Thy divine grace so that I may enjoy Thy promises. They will bring me out of sadness and guide me securely to Thy celestial tabernacle.
4. Having interest therein, I will approach the divine altar, and even to my God, Who will restore to me the gladness that rejoiced my youth.
5. There I will sing the divine praises. Why, my soul, having such a hope, art thou sad?
6. Have confidence in thy God, for I hope to go one day to bless Him and to thank Him forever in Heaven, saying to Him: Thou art my God and the delight of my eyes. For there I shall see Thee face to face, and seeing Thee will be my beatitude.

The psalm is concluded with the doxology: **"Glory be to the Father, and to the Son, and to the Holy Ghost. As it was in the beginning, is now, and ever shall be, world without end. Amen."** Fully determined to approach the altar, the priest again repeats the verse: **"I will go unto the altar of God. To God, Who giveth joy to my youth."** The celebrant then makes the Sign of the Cross, saying: **"Our help is in the name of the Lord."** To which the server replies: **"Who made Heaven and earth."**

The Confiteor

In reciting the prayers at the foot of the altar, the priest in the first place expresses a wish to approach the altar. But taking into account his great unworthiness, he is disturbed and humbled in mind. Then again, contemplating the Lord his God, he is filled with hope, and implores His assistance and mercy. To more effectually obtain these graces, he humbly confesses his sins. Bowing low, the priest recites the **Confiteor**, or general confession. In this prayer he acknowledges his sins to God, to the Saints in Heaven, and to the faithful there present. He begs their prayers for himself. At the conclusion of the **Confiteor,** the server in the name of the people says: **"May Almighty God have mercy upon you, forgive you your sins, and bring you to everlasting life"**—to which the priest responds, **"Amen,"** that is, "May your prayer be granted."

Hereupon the server repeats the **Confiteor** in the name of the people. The object of saying the **Confiteor** at the beginning of Mass is to prepare both priest and people for the great Sacrifice by the sincere repentance of their sins. "Why," someone may ask, "do you make confession to the Saints and to one another? Is it not sufficient to confess them to God?" This practice is based upon Scripture. In *James* 5:16, we read: "Confess therefore, your sins one to another: and pray one for another, that you may be saved. For the continual prayer of a just man availeth much." Speaking of the prayers at the foot of the altar, Chateaubriand in his *Genius of Christianity* says that if it occurred in a Greek tragedy, the philosopher would admire the idyllic dialogue with which the Christian Sacrifice opens, in which the priest, bowed down by the weight of years and experience, groans over the misery of sinful man, while the server, full of youth and hope, bids him take courage to mount the altar.

The **Confiteor**, so-called from the first word, ***"Confiteor,"*** **"I confess,"** is a general confession of sins. When reciting the **Confiteor,** the celebrant and servers bow down their heads in shame and humility. At the words, **"through my fault,"** etc. the speaker strikes his breast three times. This gesture is indicative of sorrow and is made in imitation of the publican mentioned in the Gospel, who "struck his breast saying: O God, be merciful to me a sinner." (*Luke* 18:13).

In the Old as well as in the New Law, the confession of sins has invariably preceded sacrifice. In the Old Testament, before the High Priest offered the emissary goat, he was directed to "confess all the iniquities of the children of Israel, and all their offenses and sins." (*Lev*. 16:21). The reciting of the **Confiteor** reminds us that Christ vouchsafed to charge Himself with our sins.

After the humble acknowledgment of unworthiness on the part of the celebrant and the congregation expressed in the words of the **Confiteor**, the priest raises his head and signs himself with the Sign of the Cross, saying: **"May the almighty and merciful Lord grant us pardon, absolution and remission of our sins."** To this the server responds: **"Amen."** Asking for pardon, the priest appeals to the omnipotence and to the mercy of God. In God's omnipotence we find the secret of His mercy. How childlike and pathetic is the following prayer of the priest: **"O God, Thou wilt turn again and quicken us,"** and the response of the congregation voiced by the server: **"And Thy people shall rejoice in Thee."** And the pleading of the penitent sinner with the merciful God continues: **"Show us, O Lord, Thy mercy."** The desire of the yearning soul for union with God is expressed in the response of the server: **"And grant us Thy salvation."** One more appeal goes forth from the heart of the priest to the heart of God: **"O Lord, hear my prayer." "And let my cry come unto Thee,"** the altar boy pleads in the name of the people.

Beautiful and pathetic are these prayers uttered by the priest and server at the foot of the altar, and well calculated to fill the heart with sentiments of true sorrow and filial confidence. To participate in the drama which is enacted at the altar, the people, who are represented by the server, should give expression interiorly to similar sentiments.

Ascending the Altar

The priest slowly ascends the altar steps praying.

Let us pray: Take away from us our iniquities, we beseech Thee, O Lord, that we may be worthy to enter with pure minds into the Holy of Holies. Through Christ our Lord. Amen.

In the greeting that is exchanged between the priest and people, divine assistance was invoked for devout prayer, to which all are invited by the word

***"Oremus"*—"Let us pray,"** which is uttered by the celebrant in a loud voice. The invitation is emphasized by the priest extending his hands, as if inviting all. The celebrant now stands erect ready to ascend the altar, that mystical Calvary on which he, like Moses on Mount Sinai, is privileged to be nearer to God than is the assembled congregation. Realizing this he goes up to the altar; and as he advances, full of holy fear, he says in a low tone: **"Take away from us our sins,"** etc. As by the descending of the priest from the altar we are reminded of the fall of man and the loss of God's friendship through sin, so by the priest's ascending we are reminded of our restoration to God's favor through the Passion of Christ.

Kissing the Altar

The priest bows and kisses the altar.

We beseech Thee, O Lord, by the merits of Thy Saints whose relics are here, and of all the Saints, that Thou wouldst vouchsafe to forgive me all my sins. Amen.

Arrived at the altar, the priest bows and kisses it. This is done 1) out of respect to the altar which has been consecrated by the bishop through prayer and the word of God; 2) out of respect to the Body and Blood of Christ which rests in the tabernacle upon the altar; 3) out of respect to the Saints, relics of whom are preserved in the altarstone; 4) out of respect to Christ, Who is symbolized by the altar. This ceremony reminds us that in order to assist worthily at this Sacrifice we must put aside all malice and hatred and be united with the bond of Christian charity.

The Mass is the unbloody renewal of the bloody Sacrifice on the Cross. The blood of Christ was shed unto the remission of sins. But the merits of this precious blood-shedding must be applied to the individual soul. This explains that constant cry for mercy which is expressed in this prayer and so many other prayers of the Mass.

The Introit

The priest proceeds to the Missal.

Blessed be the Holy Trinity and undivided Unity. We will give glory to Him, because He hath shown His mercy to us. (*Tob.* 12). O Lord, our Lord, how excellent is Thy Name in all the earth. (*Ps.* 8). Glory be to the Father, and to the Son, and to the Holy Ghost. As it was in the beginning, is now, and ever shall be, world without end. Amen.

Blessed be the Holy Trinity and undivided Unity. We will give glory to Him, because He hath shown His mercy to us. (This is the Introit used on Trinity Sunday. The Introit varies with the feast.)

The **Introit** is the first prayer which the priest reads from the Missal at the right, or Epistle side, of the altar. **The Introit,** which is derived from the Latin word ***introitus,*** meaning **"entrance,"** is so called because formerly, it was customary to chant this prayer when the priest advanced toward the altar, or when the people entered the church. It consists of a text selected from the Bible and terminates with the doxology, **"Glory be to the Father,"** etc. The **Introit** varies from day to day in accordance with the feast that is celebrated.

The recital of the **Introit** should be considered as the real beginning of Mass, since what has gone before is rather of the nature of the celebrant's preparation. For this reason the priest makes the Sign of the Cross at its first words, according to the general rule of beginning all solemn functions with that sign. At Requiem Masses—Masses for the Dead—he makes the cross not on himself but over the Missal. This is understood as directing the blessing to the souls in Purgatory. The reciting of the Introit reminds us of the ancient world's sighing for the Redeemer and begging God to hasten His advent. It should awaken within us a great esteem for this same Redeemer, Whom, happily, we possess, and whose benefits we enjoy in the present Sacrifice. The priest repeats the **Introit** to mark the holy impatience of the Patriarchs and the frequent prayers they made to God to send the Redeemer.

The Kyrie

The priest returns to the center of the altar for the Kyrie.

P. Lord, have mercy on us. ***(Kyrie eleison.)***
S. Lord, have mercy on us. ***(Kyrie eleison.)***
P. Lord, have mercy on us. ***(Kyrie eleison.)***
S. Christ, have mercy on us. ***(Christe eleison.)***
P. Christ, have mercy on us. ***(Christe eleison.)***
S. Christ, have mercy on us. ***(Christe eleison.)***
P. Lord, have mercy on us. ***(Kyrie eleison.)***
S. Lord, have mercy on us. ***(Kyrie eleison.)***
P. Lord, have mercy on us. ***(Kyrie eleison.)***

After reading the Introit, the priest returns to the middle of the altar to recite the **Kyrie Eleison** before the altar crucifix. It is a cry for mercy. ***"Kyrie Eleison"*** is addressed three times to God the Father. Then, ***"Christe eleison"*** is said thrice to God the Son. The ***"Kyrie eleison"*** is again said three times, this time to God the Holy Ghost. In this most simple and, at the same time, most beautiful prayer, we implore the three Divine Persons to grant us mercy and pardon. Such a petition is most appropriately recited at the commencement of this tremendous Sacrifice.

To the Father and the Holy Ghost we say ***"Kyrie eleison,"*** and to the Son, ***"Christe eleison."*** Pope Innocent III gives this reason for this practice: "The Father and Holy Ghost have only the Divine nature. But in the Son there is a double nature, the Divine and human. To call attention to the Son's human nature we address Him as ***Christe,*** that is, **'Anointed.'** In the second Person of the Blessed Trinity the human nature was ***anointed,*** united, with the Divine." (*Lib.* II., *de Myster. Miss., cap.* 19).

"Kyrie Eleison" are two Greek words which signify **"Lord, have mercy!"** This is the only prayer of the Mass which is recited in the Greek language. It was introduced into the western Church from the Orient and, on account of its frequent use at the various religious services, became very popular. On account of its peculiar emphasis and venerable antiquity it was not translated into Latin. By this the Latin Church also shows her Catholicity and the communion of all the congregations of the faithful throughout the universe, and how every tongue confesses the Lord Jesus Christ. Since, besides this Greek prayer, the Church has retained in the liturgy the Hebrew expressions ***Amen,***

Alleluia, Sabaoth and ***Hosanna,*** we find her employing at the altar of the unbloody Sacrifice the three languages used in writing the inscription which was fixed to the Cross on which Christ offered His bloody Sacrifice.

The Gloria

The priest, standing in the center, recites the Gloria.

Glory to God in the highest, and on earth, peace to men of good will. We praise Thee. We bless Thee. We adore Thee. We glorify Thee. We give Thee thanks for Thy great glory. O Lord God, heavenly King, God the Father Almighty. O Lord Jesus Christ, the only-begotten Son. Lord God, Lamb of God, Son of the Father. Thou Who takest away the sins of the world, have mercy on us. Thou Who takest away the sins of the world, receive our prayer. Thou Who sittest at the right hand of the Father, have mercy on us. For Thou alone art holy. Thou alone art the Lord. Thou alone, O Jesus Christ, art most high. With the Holy Ghost, ✠ in the glory of God the Father. Amen.

Immediately after the **Kyrie** follows the **Gloria.** This magnificent prayer is not so much a supplication as the exultation of praise. It is called the "Angelic Hymn" because it commences with the words chanted by angelic voices at the birth of our Redeemer. This birth was announced to the shepherds by an angel with whom there was "a multitude of the heavenly army, praising God, and saying: Glory to God in the highest ***(Gloria in excelsis Deo),*** and on earth peace to men of good will." (*Luke* 2:13). This canticle consists of the strain sung by the multitude of the heavenly army, and of pious aspirations composed by the Church. It is also called the **Great Doxology** or hymn of praise.

When the priest commences this hymn, he stretches out and elevates his hands and turns his eyes toward Heaven. A pious sensibility naturally suggests such gestures. They exhibit in a feeling manner those profound inward emotions and that religious elevation of the soul experienced by the fervent Christian, and testify that while his lips are resounding with those angelic notes of praise, "Glory to God in the highest," they but echo the accent of a heart that sighs to embrace and retain the joys of Heaven for all eternity.

The inclinations of the head at the Name of God manifest our worship of God, Who was made man for our redemption. At the conclusion the priest makes the Sign of the Cross, according to the custom of the ancient Christians, who sanctified all their principal actions by calling to mind the sacrifice of Christ on the Cross. The **Gloria,** being a canticle of gladness, is omitted at Masses said in black for the dead, and also during the penitential seasons of Advent and Lent, unless the Mass be said in honor of some saint.

The Dominus Vobiscum

The priest kisses the altar and turns to the people.

P. The Lord be with you. ***(Dominus vobiscum.)***
S. And with thy spirit. ***(Et cum spiritu tuo.)***

At the end of the **Gloria** the priest bows down, kisses the altar and turns to the people, saying: **"The Lord be with you,"** to which the server responds: **"And with**

thy spirit." The priest bows down before the altar because he who wishes to communicate a benediction unto others must first of all, by his humility, incline Heaven to bestow the blessing which he desires to impart. He kisses the altar because it is the throne of Jesus. He faces the congregation because with the words, ***"Dominus vobiscum,"*** he greets the people. He holds his arms extended to signify by such a natural expression of sincere and warm affection that he is acting in the name of Jesus, the loving Shepherd of the Fold, Who died on the Cross with outstretched arms in token of His readiness to receive all sinners who are truly penitent. To the greeting of the priest, the server, in the name of the people, again responds: **"And with thy spirit."** The Church intends, by this frequent interchange of holy affections between the priest and the people, to excite devotion and to teach us how we should desire above all things to remain always in the peace of God.

***"Dominus vobiscum"*—"The Lord be with you"** is a salutation which is frequently repeated at Catholic services. It is a greeting which comprises every good that the Church could possibly wish her children, for "if the Lord be with us, who can be against us?" This greeting is also met with in Holy Scripture. (*Ruth* 2:4; cf. also *Luke* 1:28, *1 Cor.* 16:23). The people have just voiced their earnest desire that their prayer for mercy and forgiveness be acceptable to God. Thereupon the priest, acting as mediator, expresses his wish that their prayer may find favor with God; he says: **"The Lord be with you."** It would be proper to answer in these words: "May the Lord, likewise, be with you." The people, however, do not reply after this manner, but say instead: ***"Et cum spiritu tuo"*—"And [may the Lord**

be] with thy spirit" (cf. *Phil.* 4:23)—that is to say, "May the Lord be with your soul, in your mind, and in your heart." Because this divine work is chiefly spiritual and refers to the soul, therefore it is petitioned that the Lord fill the *soul* of the priest with His abundant graces.

The Collect

The priest returns to the Missal and reads the Collect.

Let us pray: Almighty and everlasting God, Who hast granted to Thy servants, in the confession of the true Faith, to acknowledge the glory of the eternal Trinity and to adore the Unity in the power of Thy Majesty; grant that, by steadfastness in the same Faith, we may ever be defended from all adversities. Through Jesus Christ, Thy Son our Lord, Who liveth and reigneth with Thee in the unity of the Holy Ghost, world without end. Amen. (This Collect is proper for Trinity Sunday.)

Having greeted the people, the priest returns to the Epistle side of the altar and from the Missal, with extended arms, reads the **"Collects,"*** or **Prayers** of the day. He begins these prayers with the invitation, ***"Oremus"*—"Let us pray."** He thus asks the people to join him in his prayers.

The priest prays with extended arms in imitation of Moses, who prayed thus upon the mountain while the children of Israel were contending with the Amalekites on the plain. Nothing can be more impres-

* Col´lect. The first syllable is accented.

sive than this scriptural custom of praying with extended arms. The Psalmist makes frequent mention of it. He says: "Hear, O Lord, the voice of my supplication, when I pray to Thee; when I lift my hands to Thy holy Temple." (*Ps*. 27:2).

In the early days of Christianity the word "Collect" was used to signify a meeting of the faithful for prayer. It was usual for the people to assemble in a particular church on fast days, but especially in time of public calamity, and from there they would proceed in regular procession to another church, previously determined. When the clergy and the people had assembled at the place appointed, the bishop or the priest who was to officiate recited over the assembled multitude a short prayer, which, from the circumstance, was called the **Collect**, or the gathering prayer. Before the celebrant began the prayer itself, he exhorted—as he does today—the people to offer their petitions to God, saying: ***"Oremus"*****—"Let us pray."** The deacon then proclaimed aloud: ***"Flectamus genua"*****—"Let us kneel";** after a short time, during which all present prayed silently, he cried out a second time: ***"Levate"*****—"Arise,"** whereupon the priest, rising from his knees, prayed aloud.

These prayers are appropriately called **"Collects"** also because they contain the sum and substance of all favors asked by the priest for himself and for the people. They are usually directed to the Father, to Whom the Sacrifice of the Son is offered, and terminate with the words: *"Per Dominum nostrum Jesum Christum"*— "Through Jesus Christ our Lord." These words declare Christ to be the only mediator through Whose divine merits and mercy we have the hope of having all our petitions heard. When the priest says these words he bows to the altar crucifix, thereby paying reverence to Jesus Christ, Who is represented and called to mind by the crucifix.

The acolyte answers **"Amen"** at the end of the **Collect,** thus expressing approval and ratifying what the priest has been saying. ***"Amen"*** is a Hebrew word employed to confirm what has been announced. It may signify, **"That is true,"** or **"May it be so,"** or **"I agree to that."**

The number of **Collects** is not the same at all Masses. When there are more than one, the second **Collect** begins also with ***Oremus,*** and all that follow are joined together without intermediate ending or ***Oremus.*** The ending, ***"Per Dominum nostrum,"*** etc., is then added to the last **Collect**. In this way the **Collect** of the day is separated from the others and is given a special dignity. The total number of **Collects** must be an uneven one and never exceed seven. **One** signifies God's Unity; **three**, His Trinity; **five**, Christ's wounds; **seven**, the gifts of the Holy Ghost.

The Epistle

The priest reads the Epistle, his hands resting on the Missal stand.

P. O the depth of the riches of the wisdom and of the knowledge of God! How incomprehensible are His judgments, and how unsearchable His ways! For who hath known the mind of the Lord? Or who hath been His counsellor? Or who hath first given to Him, and recompense shall be made him? For of Him, and by Him, and in Him, are all things: to Him be glory forever. Amen. (*Rom.* 11:33-36. This is the Epistle for Trinity Sunday).

S. Thanks be to God. ***(Deo Gratias.)***

After the Collects, the priest reads the **Epistle. Epistle** means "letter." It is not only by prayer, but also by pious readings that the faithful are prepared for the Holy Sacrifice. The Jews commenced the public service of their Sabbath by reading the books of Moses and the Prophets. The first Christians followed this example. Before celebrating the Sacred Mysteries on Sundays, they would read passages from the Old or New Testament. But as these selections were generally taken from the letters of St. Paul, this Scriptural reading was popularly called the **"Epistle."** Our Sunday **Epistles** are taken chiefly from the letters of St. Paul or of the other Apostles. The **Epistle** is read before the **Gospel,** because it is the utterance of the Apostles. The **Gospel** is the word of Christ Himself, and it is proper that by the voice of His ministers we should be prepared to listen to the Master Himself. Moreover, by this arrangement the Church appears to follow the example of Christ, Who sent some of His disciples before Him into those quarters which He was about to honor with a visit.

When the **Epistle** is ended, the server answers, ***"Deo gratias,"*** that is to say, **"Thanks be to God"** for the good instruction contained in the **Epistle.**

The **Epistle** reminds us of the life and teaching of Christ made known to us by the Apostles and Prophets.

The Gradual and Alleluia or Tract, and the Sequences

The priest reads the Gradual.

Blessed art Thou, O Lord, Who beholdest the depths and sittest upon the Cherubim.

Blessed art Thou, O Lord, in the firmament of heaven, and worthy of praise for ever. (From *Dan.* 3:55-56). (Gradual for Trinity Sunday).

Alleluia, alleluia. Blessed art Thou, O Lord God of our fathers, and worthy of praise forever. Alleluia. (Alleluia for Trinity Sunday).

After the Epistle, in order to unite prayer with instruction, the whole or part of a Psalm is recited. This prayer is called the **Gradual (*gradus,*** "a step"), from an ancient custom of chanting these prayers from the ***gradus,*** that is, *steps* of the *ambo,* or pulpit, from which the Epistle was read. The Psalms or portions of Psalms read at this part of the Mass are an inheritance from the service of the Synagogue. Copied from that service, alternate readings and Psalms filled up a great part of the first half of the sacred service which today we call the Mass. St. Augustine mentions this practice: "We have heard first the lesson from the Apostle (Epistle). Then we sang a Psalm (Gradual). After that, the lesson of the Gospel." (*Serm.* 176).

The versicles comprising the **Gradual** were sometimes chanted by one chorister alone, without any pause, and sometimes alternately by many voices. When the chanting was performed by one person and without interruption, it was called **Tract**, from the Latin word

***tractim,* "without interruption."** As there is something plaintive about long-drawn-out strains of a single voice, the **Tract** is said in penitential seasons.

During Eastertide the repetition of the **Alleluia** replaces the **Gradual. Alleluia** is a Hebrew term meaning, **"Praise the Lord."** As it expresses a transport of joy which cannot be adequately rendered by any term in Latin, it has been retained in its original form. The **Alleluia** is the canticle of the heavenly Sion, which St. John heard intoned there: "After these things I heard as it were the voice of many people in heaven, saying: Alleluia. Salvation, and glory, and power is to our God." (*Apoc*. 19:1).

On certain days, after the **Gradual** has been read, the priest reads a certain poem. These poems are called **Sequences**, because they are read **following** (Latin: *sequens*) the Gradual. We have five **Sequences** in the Missal. The first is the ***Victimae Paschali*—"To the Paschal Victim,"** sung at Easter. This poem is ascribed to Robert, King of the Franks, in the eleventh century. The second is the ***Veni, Sancte Spiritus*—"Come, Holy Spirit,"** used on Pentecost, which is believed to have been composed in the eleventh century by Blessed Hermanus Contractus. The third is the ***Lauda Sion*—"Praise, O Sion,"** for the Feast of Corpus Christi. This composition is ascribed to St. Thomas Aquinas. The fourth is the ***Dies Irae*—"Day of Wrath,"** recited at Requiem Masses. It is generally ascribed to Thomas of Celano, who died around A. D. 1260. The fifth is the ***Stabat Mater*—"The Mother Stood,"** attributed to Pope Innocent III. It is recited on the Feast of the Seven Dolors.

After the reading of the **Gradual** or **Tract,** the server carries the Missal to the left or Gospel side of the altar. According to an old custom, church and altar should be erected in such a manner that the priest faces the East (*ad orientem*) when offering Mass. If this custom is followed, the priest will face toward North when reading the Gospel. As the South, with its luxuriant vegetation, was regarded as a *type* of the realm of grace, so the cold North, with its extensive wastes, came to be regarded as the realm of evil. Before the glad tidings were announced on that first Christmas night, this world was steeped in cold materialism. But when the Gospel of Christ was preached, the face of the earth was renewed, and love for God and for virtue was re-enkindled in the hearts of men.

The Jews, to whom the "Gospel of the Kingdom" was first preached, rejected it. It was then carried to the Gentiles. This is symbolized by carrying the Missal to the other side of the altar. Transferring the Missal from one side of the altar to the other also recalls to our minds how Our Lord was led about from one iniquitous judge to another.

The Munda Cor Meum

The priest goes to the center of the altar, bows down and prays.

Cleanse my heart and my lips, O Almighty God, Who didst cleanse the lips of the prophet Isaias with a burning coal: and vouchsafe, through Thy gracious mercy, so to purify me that I may worthily proclaim Thy holy Gospel. Through Christ our Lord. Amen.

Be pleased, O Lord, to give Thy blessing.

The Lord be in my heart and on my lips, that I may worthily, and in a becoming manner, announce His holy Gospel.

While the Missal is being transferred, the priest proceeds to the middle of the altar, where he makes a profound bow and asks God to purify his heart and lips, as He once did those of the Prophet Isaias with a burning coal, and enable him worthily to announce the Gospel to the people. The people, in the meantime, pray that they may listen to the word of God attentively and with benefit.

The allusion to Isaias in this prayer recalls to mind the Prophet's wonderful vision. He had been granted a vision of the glories of Heaven. He is overcome with humility at the thought of his unworthiness and exclaims: "Woe is me . . . because I am a man of unclean lips . . . and I have seen with my eyes the King the Lord of hosts." In answer to his prayer he was purified by the grace of God: "And one of the seraphim flew to me, and in his hand was a live coal, which he had taken with the tongs off the altar. And he touched my mouth, and said: Behold this hath touched thy lips, and thy iniquities shall be taken away, and thy sin shall be cleansed." (*Is.* 6:5-7).

When the priest proceeds to the Missal to read the Gospel, the people arise. By this they signify their readiness to stand up for and defend Christ's teaching. This practice also reminds the faithful that through the Gospel of Christ, man is raised up from sin to newness of life.

The Gospel

The priest reads the Gospel.

P. The Lord be with you. *(Dominus vobiscum.)*

S. And with thy spirit. *(Et cum spiritu tuo.)*

P. The continuation of the holy Gospel according to St. Matthew. *(Sequentia sancti Evangelii secun-*

dum Matthaeum.)
S. Glory be to Thee, O Lord. ***(Gloria tibi, Domine.)***

P. At that time Jesus said to His disciples: All power is given to Me in heaven and on earth. Going, therefore, teach ye all nations, baptizing them in the name of the Father, and of the Son, and of the Holy Ghost, teaching them to observe all things whatsoever I have commanded you. And behold I am with you all days, even to the consummation of the world. (*Matt.* 28:18-20). (Gospel for Trinity Sunday).

P. Through the words of the Gospel may our sins be blotted out.
S. Praise be to Thee, O Christ. ***(Laus tibi, Christe.)***

Having finished the prayer at the middle of the altar, the priest proceeds to the Missal, which is now on the left side of the altar, to read the **Gospel.** "Gospel" is an Anglo-Saxon word composed of the word **God** and **spell**, a story or narrative. The **Gospel** is a selection from one of the four Evangelists—Matthew, Mark, Luke and John—and it varies according to the feast of the day. During the reading of the Gospel the people stand as a sign of reverence for the word of God and a willingness to follow it.

Before reading the **Gospel** the priest again says: ***"Dominus vobiscum."*** After the response of the server, he announces from which Evangelist the Gospel of the day is taken by saying: ***"Sequentia sancti Evangelii secundum Matthaeum"*** (or ***Lucam,*** or ***Marcum,*** or ***Joannem,*** as the case may be), that is, **"The continuation of the holy Gospel according to St. Matthew."** Hereupon the acolyte answers: ***"Gloria tibi, Domine"—*** **"Glory be to Thee, O Lord."** Saying this last sentence, the priest makes the Sign of the Cross on the Missal with his thumb to signify that the Gospel he is about to read is the word of Christ crucified, Who died for the truth of His doctrine. At the words ***"Gloria tibi, Domine,"*** he makes the Sign of the Cross with his thumb on his forehead, on his lips, and on his breast. The people imitate this ceremony. Making this threefold Sign of the Cross, we ask God for the grace to know His teaching with our minds, to profess it with our lips and love it and follow it with all our heart.

At the end of the Gospel the priest kisses the book. This is done out of reverence for the word of God and to signify that everything which emanates from such a hallowed source is sweet and venerable. When kissing the sacred text the priest says: **"Through the words of the Gospel may our sins be blotted out."** The server says, in the name of the people, ***"Laus tibi, Christe"—*** **"Praise be to Thee, O Christ."** With this sentence the people express their devotion for Christ, inspired by the reading of His word.

On Sundays and holy days of obligation a sermon is usually preached in explanation of the **Gospel.** (The sermon is not actually part of the Mass.)

The Credo (Creed)

The priest returns to the center of the altar.

I believe in one God, the Father Almighty, maker of heaven and earth, and of all things visible and invisible. And in one Lord Jesus Christ, the only begotten Son of God, and born of the Father before all ages. God of God, Light of Light, true God of true God; begotten, not made, consubstantial with the

Father, by Whom all things were made. Who for us men, and for our salvation, came down from heaven. *(Kneel)* And became incarnate by the Holy Spirit of the Virgin Mary, AND WAS MADE MAN. *(Arise)* He was also crucified for us, suffered under Pontius Pilate and was buried, and the third day He rose again according to the Scriptures. And He ascended into heaven: He sitteth at the right hand of the Father. And He shall come again with glory to judge both the living and the dead; of Whose Kingdom there shall be no end. And I believe in the Holy Ghost, the Lord and Giver of life, Who proceedeth from the Father and the Son; Who together with the Father and the Son is adored and glorified; Who spoke by the Prophets. And in one holy, Catholic and Apostolic Church. I confess one baptism for the remission of sins; and I look for the resurrection of the dead, and ✠ the life of the world to come. Amen.

After the Gospel, the profession of faith follows. The priest returns to the center of the altar. He stretches out and elevates his hands, turns his eyes toward Heaven and says the prayer which begins with the word, ***"Credo"*****—"I believe."** This is the answer of the Church to the Gospel teaching. She replies that she believes all whatsoever Christ taught. The **Credo** is an abridgment of the Christian doctrine and is often called the *Symbol* of Faith. "Symbol" means a sign used to distinguish one thing from another. To the first Christians the Symbol or **Credo** was what the watchword is now to an army in the field, a signal by which a friend may be distinguished from a foe. As the **Creed** was the medium through which the true believer was recognized amid unbelievers, it became customary to say: *"Da Symbolum"*—"Give the Symbol."

The formula used at Mass is known as the **Nicene Creed.** It is the profession of faith which was made by the universal Church assembled in council at Nicea in the year 325 and amplified at the Council of Constantinople in the year 381. Besides this formula there are three others which are often used by the Church at various functions: the **Apostles' Creed,** considered to have been drawn up by the Apostles; the **Athanasian Creed,** considered to have been composed by St. Athanasius, setting forth principally the doctrine of the Trinity; and the **Tridentine Creed,** or Creed of Pius IV, containing the teachings of the Council of Trent and published in 1564.

While reciting the Creed the priest inclines his head as he pronounces the name of God. He does this to show his respect for the name of God. At the words ***"Et incarnatus est de Spiritu Sancto ex Maria Virgine: ET HOMO FACTUS EST"*—"And became incarnate by the Holy Spirit of the Virgin Mary: AND WAS MADE MAN,"** the priest and people bend the knee in reverence to the mystery of the Incarnation and to **adore** God made man, "who being in the form of God, thought it not robbery to be equal with God: but emptied Himself, taking the form of a servant, being made in the likeness of men . . . for which cause God also hath exalted Him, and hath given Him a Name which is above all names: that in the Name of Jesus every knee should bow, of those that are in Heaven, on earth, and under the earth." (*Phil.* 2:6-10). By kneeling down in gratitude to the Son of God for having become man for us and rising again, we express our hope of a joyful resurrection.

On days of the week on which no feast occurs, or

when the feast is that of a martyr, confessor, virgin or widow, the **Credo** is not said; nor is it said in Masses for the dead.

In former times, as soon as the Credo was finished, all who had not been baptized, or were under a course of penance, or had not been admitted to Communion, were ordered to leave the church. This was the end of the "Mass of the Catechumens." That which followed—"The Mass of the Faithful"—was considered too holy for the presence of notorious sinners and too mysterious to permit those to assist who were not yet fully instructed. The Church has changed her discipline in this regard, and she now permits all to remain during the whole of the sacred rite.

Chapter 2

The Offertory, The First of the Three Principal Parts of the Mass

The Preparation of the Sacrifice

During this part of the Mass, preparation is made for the Sacrifice. The offerings of bread and wine are blessed and dedicated in order that at the Consecration they may become the Body and Blood of Christ. Pope Innocent III says: "After listening to the Gospel there should follow, not only faith in heart (which is evidenced by reciting the Creed), but above all fruit in work, manifested by our gifts."

The priest kisses the altar, then, turning to the people, he says:

P. The Lord be with you. *(Dominus vobiscum.)*
S. And with thy spirit. *(Et cum spiritu tuo.)*

The Offertory Antiphon

The priest reads the Offertory Antiphon.

P. Let us pray: Blessed be God the Father, and the only-begotten Son of God, and also the Holy Spirit;

because He hath shown His mercy to us. (Offertory Antiphon for Trinity Sunday).

THE OFFERTORY

The priest removes the veil from the Chalice. 

Offering the bread, the priest prays:

Accept, O holy Father, Almighty and Eternal God, this spotless Host, which I, Thy unworthy servant, offer unto Thee, my living and true God, for my innumerable sins, offenses and negligences, and for all here present; as also for all faithful Christians, both living and dead, that it may be profitable for my own and for their salvation unto life eternal. Amen.

Pouring wine and water into the chalice and blessing the water:

O God, ✠ Who in creating human nature didst wonderfully dignify it, and hast still more wonderfully renewed it; grant that by the mystery of this water and wine, we may be made partakers of His divinity, Who vouchsafed to become partaker of our humanity, Jesus Christ, Thy Son, our Lord, Who liveth and reigneth with Thee in the unity of the Holy Ghost, God, world without end. Amen.

Offering the chalice:

We offer unto Thee, O Lord, the chalice of salvation, humbly begging Thy mercy, that it may ascend with an odor of sweetness in the sight of Thy Divine

---

The Server rings a small handbell at certain important parts of the Mass.

Majesty, for our salvation and for that of the whole world. Amen.

Bowing down in the center of the altar:

In the spirit of humility and with a contrite heart, may we be received by Thee, O Lord; and grant that the sacrifice we offer in Thy sight this day may be pleasing to Thee, O Lord God.

Blessing the bread and wine:

Come, O Sanctifier, Almighty and Eternal God, and bless ✠ this sacrifice prepared for the glory of Thy Holy Name.

The Offertory Antiphon

After the recitation of the **Credo** the priest again kisses the altar, faces the congregation and says: **"Dominus vobiscum"—"The Lord be with you."** The server responds, ***"Et cum spiritu tuo"*—"And with your spirit."** With this greeting, priest and people express the wish that God may assist them to offer a worthy sacrifice.

Turning to the altar and extending his hands, the priest invites the people to prayer, saying, ***"Oremus"*—"Let us pray."** The **Offertory Antiphon** (also called the Offertory Verse or simply the "Offertory") is then said. It is a prayer recited by way of preparation for the oblation. The **Offertory Antiphon** is called by this name because formerly, while the people presented the bread and wine used at the sacrifice, it was customary to chant this prayer. In connection with the offering of bread and wine, the faithful also made offerings of the fruits of the field, oil, wax and, later, also money for the support of the clergy and the maintenance of divine services. The **Offertory Antiphon** varies from day to day.

The Oblation of the Bread*

Having recited the **Offertory Antiphon**, the priest uncovers the chalice and removes it from the center of the altar, placing it at his right. When the veil is being removed, the server rings the bell as a signal for the congregation to unite with the priest in offering to God the gifts of bread and wine. The pall is taken off the chalice and placed against the altar ledge. The priest then takes the unconsecrated altar bread, which we call the **host** (from the Latin *hostia,* that is, "victim"), and raising it on the paten or gilt plate, lifting it up to Heaven, offers it to Almighty God, saying this prayer: **"Accept, O holy Father,"** etc. Over the corporal he makes the Sign of the Cross with the paten, on which rests the host. At the beginning of the Mass the corporal was spread out in the center of the altar; now the priest deposits the host on the corporal and places the paten a little to the right.

The Oblation of the Chalice

Taking the chalice, the celebrant goes to the Epistle side of the altar, pours into the chalice the wine which is to be consecrated, and mixes with it a few

* Oblation—the act by which the victim of a sacrifice is offered to God. The oblation of the bread and wine in the Offertory anticipates the oblation of the *Divine Victim,* which the bread and wine will become at the Consecration. The sacrificial Gift offered to God in the Mass is the Divine Victim, Christ.

drops of water. Before taking the cruet containing the water, the priest makes the Sign of the Cross over it. It should be remembered that the Sign of the Cross is made so frequently during the celebration of the Mass, and in blessing anything dedicated to the service of Almighty God, in order to indicate that all our hopes of obtaining the blessings prayed for are founded solely on the merits of Christ's Passion and death on the Cross. Only the water is here blessed, and not the wine. The reason is this: The wine signifies Christ, Who needs no benediction. But the water represents human nature, which, with its frailties, has great need of God's blessing.

A little water is mixed with the wine in accordance with the tradition of the Church, which teaches us that water was mingled with the wine at the Last Supper. This ceremony reminds us that the Son of God took to Himself our human nature and makes us sharers in His Divine nature by Sanctifying Grace. It also recalls to mind the fact that blood and water flowed from our Saviour's side when He was pierced with the lance.

Returning to the center of the altar with the chalice and raising it to Heaven, the priest now offers to God the wine, which will soon be changed into Our Lord's Precious Blood, saying: **"We offer unto Thee, O Lord, the chalice of salvation, humbly begging Thy mercy, that it may ascend with an odor of sweetness in the sight of Thy Divine Majesty, for our salvation and for that of the whole world. Amen."** Before placing the chalice on the corporal, he makes with it the Sign of the Cross and then covers it with the pall.

Bowing low before the altar, the priest now makes the following prayer for himself and for the people: **"In the spirit of humility,"** etc.

All is now ready for the Sacrifice. First the bread, next the wine, and lastly the hearts of the people have been separately offered up to God. Then, as nothing is ever done in the order of grace without the help of the Holy Spirit, the priest prays, while extending his arms and making the Sign of the Cross over the bread and wine: **"Come, O Sanctifier, Almighty and Eternal God, and bless ✠ this sacrifice prepared for the glory of Thy Holy Name."**

The Lavabo

The priest goes to the side and washes his hands.

Washing his hands:

I will wash my hands among the innocent, and will encompass Thy altar, O Lord.

That I may hear the voice of praise, and tell of all Thy marvelous works.

I have loved, O Lord, the beauty of Thy house, and the place where Thy glory dwelleth.

Take not away my soul, O God, with the wicked, nor my life with men of blood.

In whose hands are iniquities; their right hand is filled with gifts.

As for me, I have walked in my innocence; redeem me, and have mercy upon me.

My foot hath stood in the right path. In the churches I will bless Thee, O Lord.

Glory be to the Father, and to the Son, and to the Holy Ghost.

As it was in the beginning, is now, and ever shall be, world without end. Amen.

Bowing before the altar:

Receive, O Holy Trinity, this oblation, which we offer Thee in memory of the Passion, Resurrection and Ascension of Our Lord Jesus Christ, in honor of the Blessed Mary ever Virgin, of blessed John the Baptist, and of the Holy Apostles Peter and Paul, and of these* and of all the Saints, that it may tend to their honor and to our salvation, and that they, whose memory we celebrate upon earth, may deign to intercede for us in Heaven, through the same Christ Our Lord. Amen.

Having made the oblation of the bread and wine, the priest retires to the Epistle side of the altar and there washes his fingers. While doing this he recites the twenty-fifth psalm, beginning at the sixth verse with the words: **"I will wash my hands among the innocent,"** etc. This ceremony is called the **Lavabo** because the Latin equivalent for **"I will wash"** is ***"Lavabo."*** This rite, the washing of the hands, is often met with in the Scriptures as an emblem of purity. It is with great propriety, therefore, that the Church has adopted into her service a ceremony so expressive of the innocence and purity with which we ought to approach the great Sacrifice of the New Law.

Since the priest washes his hands in the sacristy before vesting for Mass, it may be asked: Why this second washing after the Offertory? The reason for the second washing, that during the Mass, must be sought in the early centuries of the Church. It was customary for the celebrant and the deacons to receive the loaves of bread and vessels of wine from the people at

---

* The Saints whose relics are in the altar stone.

the Offertory. Hence there was a special need for this function, the washing of the hands, after the long ceremony in the ancient Church.

At the end of the Psalm recited at the **Lavabo,** the priest adds: **"Glory be to the Father,"** etc. As this is a hymn of joy, it is properly omitted in Masses for the dead and at the time when the suffering and death of Christ are commemorated (that is, during Passion Week and Holy Week).

Having performed this ablution or washing, the priest returns to the center of the altar and, bowing down his head, prays in silence for a short time. This prayer is addressed to the Holy Trinity: **"Receive, O Holy Trinity,"** etc.

The Orate Fratres

The priest faces the people and says: Orate Fratres.

P. Pray, brethren, that my sacrifice and yours may be acceptable to God the Father Almighty.

S. May the Lord receive the Sacrifice from thy hands, to the praise and glory of His Name, to our benefit, and to that of all His holy Church.

P. Amen.

By the foregoing prayer the celebrant again commends the Sacrifice to God, explaining the end for which it is offered. He next kisses the altar, turns toward the people and with outstretched arms solicits their prayers, saying aloud, ***"Orate, Fratres"*****—"Pray, brethren,"** and turning again to the altar he continues, **"that my sacrifice and yours may be acceptable to God the Father Almighty."**

To this invitation from the celebrant to the congregation to pray, the server answers in the name of all the people: **"May the Lord receive the Sacrifice from thy hands,"** etc.

At the **Orate Fratres** the priest turns toward the people for the last time till the Sacrifice is accomplished and Communion received. The reason is that he now enters upon the solemn part of the Mass, which includes both the Consecration and the Communion, and which therefore requires his utmost attention. He may now be considered as having taken his leave and entered, as did the High Priest of old, into the Holy of Holies. Hitherto he has prayed as one of the congregation, standing in the midst of the people, speaking aloud, that they might join with him. But now, like Moses, he leaves them at the foot of the mount while he ascends to the top to converse with God alone. Called to the performance of a ministry so much exalted above human nature, yet feeling his utter unworthiness, what can he do otherwise than turn to the people and with supplicant voice say: ***"Orate, Fratres"*—"Pray, brethren!"**

Let the faithful consider the priest as oppressed by the knowledge of his unworthiness, seeking the assistance of their prayers to support him during the tremendous Sacrifice he is about to accomplish.

The Secret

The priest prays in a low voice.

Sanctify, we beseech Thee, O Lord our God, by the invocation of Thy holy Name, the victim of this oblation, and by it make us ourselves an eternal offering

to Thee, through our Lord Jesus Christ, Thy Son, Who liveth and reigneth with Thee in the unity of the Holy Ghost, world without end. Amen. (Secret for Trinity Sunday).

The celebrant, having answered **"Amen"** to the prayer ***"Suscipiat Dominus sacrificium . . ."*****—"May the Lord receive the Sacrifice . . ."** recited by the server, says in a low voice the **Secret*** or **Secrets** in the same order as he said the **Collects**. The Secret is now said in a low voice merely because at the same time the choir is singing the **Offertory Antiphon**. The **Secrets** always correspond to the **Collects**. They are the same in number and always have reference to the same subject, that is, they commemorate the same solemnity or beg the intercession of the Saints mentioned in the **Collect**. The priest concludes the first and the last **Secret** with the words ***"Per Dominum nostrum,"*** etc.—**"Through our Lord,"** etc.

The conclusion of the last **Secret, *"Per omnia saecula saeculorum"*—"world without end,"** is said or sung aloud, forming the introduction of the **Preface**. If it is not borne in mind that the words ***"Per omnia saecula saeculorum"*****—"world without end,"** conclude the last **Secret** prayer, these words will be unintelligible. The people express their approval of the sentiments expressed by the priest in the Secret prayers by answering **"Amen"** aloud by the mouth of the server. These words are said aloud to alert the people to join interiorly in the responses of the Preface.

---

* In Latin, *Secreta,* meaning "set apart." The Secret is essentially a prayer "over the offerings set apart for the Sacrifice." *(St. Andrew Daily Missal).*

The Preface

The Preface is recited aloud or sung.

P. World without end. ***(Per omnia saecula saeculorum.)***

S. Amen. ***(Amen.)***

P. The Lord be with you. ***(Dominus vobiscum.)***

S. And with thy spirit. ***(Et cum spiritu tuo.)***

P. Lift up your hearts [to God]. ***(Sursum corda.)***

S. We have lifted them up to the Lord. ***(Habemus ad Dominum.)***

P. Let us give thanks to the Lord our God. ***(Gratias agamus Domino Deo nostro.)***

S. It is meet and just. ***(Dignum et justum est.)***

P. It is truly meet and just, right and profitable to salvation, that we should always and in all places give thanks to Thee, O holy Lord, Father Almighty, Eternal God. Who with Thine Only-begotten Son and the Holy Ghost are one God, one Lord; not in the unity of a single person, but in the Trinity of a single nature. For that which we believe on Thy revelation concerning Thy glory, that same we believe of Thy Son, and the same of the Holy Ghost, without difference or discrimination. So that in confessing the true and everlasting Godhead, we shall adore distinction in persons, oneness in being and equality in Majesty. This the Angels and Archangels, the Cherubim, too, and the Seraphim do praise; day to day they cease not to cry out as with one voice, saying: (Holy, holy, holy, etc.)

The word **Preface** is derived from the Latin words ***prae*** ("before") and ***facere*** ("to do or make"). Hence, literally, the **Preface** is that which is **done before.** This part of the service is called the **Preface** because it is the introduction to the second Principal Part of the Mass, the **Consecration** or **Canon**. The **Preface** is a solemn hymn of praise and thanksgiving recited in imitation of Our Lord, Who gave thanks before consecrating the bread and wine.

The **Preface** begins with a little dialogue. First, ***"Dominus vobiscum"*** with its answer is recited or chanted. The priest now calls upon the people to banish all earthly thoughts and to think of God alone, saying: ***"Sursum corda"*—"Lift up your hearts" [to God].** Saying these words, he elevates his hands, to impress more forcibly upon the minds of the people by such an outward sign the necessity of lifting up their hearts to God. The congregation, in response to this invitation, answers through the server: ***"Habemus ad Dominum"*—"We have lifted them up to the Lord."** Then follows the invitation to give thanks: ***"Gratias agamus Domino Deo nostro"*—"Let us give thanks to the Lord our God."** Saying these words, the celebrant joins his hands and bows his head to express, as significantly as possible, that it is the worship of the spirit which God insists upon. The people answer: ***"Dignum et justum est"*—"It is meet and just"** (namely, that we give thanks). Taking up the words which the people, by the mouth of the server, have just spoken, the priest proceeds: **"It is truly meet and just,"** etc.

It will be noticed that the **Preface** is a solemn canticle by which the hearts of those present are lifted up to the contemplation of heavenly things and to the giving of thanks to God on account of the various mysteries. To do this in a more worthy manner, the faithful are invited to join as "with one voice" ***("una voce")*** with the Angels, who honor the Majesty of God and repeat forever: **"Holy, holy, holy, Lord God of Hosts!"**

The **Preface** is not always the same. Different Prefaces commemorating different mysteries are recited on various feast days. The Roman Missal contains eleven **Prefaces**.

The Preface above is that of the **Most Holy Trinity.** This Preface is appointed to be recited or sung on Trinity Sunday and on all Sundays that have no special Preface. It is a magnificent hymn to **the most profound and sublime Mystery of our Faith.** The Mystery of the Most Holy Trinity is absolutely unfathomable to all created minds. The Preface of the Most Holy Trinity echoes the Athanasian Creed, which proclaims: "This is Catholic faith: that we worship one God in the Trinity and the Trinity in Unity."

At High Mass the **Preface** is sung by the celebrant. The chant is solemn and stately. Owing to the great antiquity of the various Prefaces, their authorship is hidden in obscurity.

The Sanctus

Bowing his head, the priest says:

Holy, holy, holy, Lord God of Hosts! Heaven and earth are filled with Thy glory. Hosanna in the highest. Blessed is He who comes in the name of the Lord. Hosanna in the highest.

The **Preface** closes with the **Sanctus.** As the Sanctus is merely a continuation of the **Preface,** the celebrant at High Mass could very well sing it himself. But one of the dramatic touches that continually adorn the liturgy was added here. The people too desire to say with the Angels: "Holy, holy, holy"; so when the celebrant comes to these words, the choir interrupts and themselves sing these words, continuing his sentence; the celebrant recites the Sanctus in a low voice.

The **Sanctus** is the canticle of the Angels which the prophet Isaias heard when he "saw the Lord sitting upon a throne high and elevated: and His train filled the Temple. Upon it stood the seraphims . . . And they cried one to another, and said: Holy, holy, holy, the Lord God of hosts, all the earth is full of His glory." (*Is*. 6:1-3). The addition "Blessed is He Who comes in the name of the Lord; Hosanna in the highest" (*Matt*. 21:9) is the acclamation with which the Jews greeted Christ upon His triumphal entry into Jerusalem. ***Sabaoth*** and ***Hosanna*** are Hebrew words. ***Sabaoth*** means **"hosts"** and refers to the countless number of Angels. The Hebrew word ***Hosanna*** is a practically untranslatable exclamation of triumph. It means literally, **"Oh, help."** The words **"Blessed is He Who comes in the name of the Lord"** announce Him Who is soon to come upon the altar to be immolated in an unbloody manner as being the same Who entered Jerusalem, that He might there shed His blood on the Cross.

To give notice to the congregation of the approaching Consecration, the server rings the bell at the **Sanctus.**

In some places, the server lights a special candle on the Epistle side of the Sanctuary after the Sanctus. This is the **Sanctus Candle** or the **Consecration Candle.** Its purpose is to give additional homage to Our Lord, Who at the Consecration will become present on the altar under the appearances of bread and wine. The Consecration Candle is extinguished after the door of the tabernacle is closed following Holy Communion.

Chapter 3

The Consecration *or* Canon, The Second of the Three Principal Parts of the Mass

The Offering of the Sacrifice

This part of the Mass is known as the **Canon.** "Canon" is a Greek word meaning **"rule."** The ceremonies and prayers thus far explained form no essential part of the Sacrifice, forming only a preparation for it. The same cannot be said of the prayers and ceremonies which follow, as they constitute the very action of the Sacrifice. These prayers are called the **Canon** because they have been laid down as a **rule** or **canon** which is to be rigidly followed by the priest who offers up the Sacrifice.

The prayers of the **Canon** are always said in a low tone. The priest has retired, as it were, into the inner sanctuary, to converse with God alone, where he continues in silent worship until the **Pater Noster.** The people realize what the priest is doing—offering sacrifice—hence it is not necessary that they should hear every prayer.

The Te Igitur

The priest raises his hands and eyes toward Heaven.
We therefore humbly pray and beseech Thee, most

merciful Father, through Jesus Christ, Thy Son our Lord, that Thou wouldst vouchsafe to accept and bless these ✠ gifts, these ✠ presents, these ✠ holy and unspotted sacrifices, which in the first place we offer Thee for Thy holy Catholic Church, to which deign to grant peace, as also to protect, unite and govern it throughout the world, together with Thy servant, our Pope, N., our Bishop, N., as also all orthodox believers and professors of the Catholic and Apostolic Faith.

Having finished the celestial canticle, ***"Sanctus, sanctus, sanctus,"*** etc., the priest raises his hands and eyes toward Heaven, makes a profound inclination and recites the first prayer of the Canon, ***"Te Igitur,"*** etc.

The priest prays with arms extended after the manner of Moses on the mountain (*Ex*. 18:9), or rather, as Christ did on the Cross. During this prayer he makes the Sign of the Cross three times over the oblation—when saying the words **"gifts," "presents"** and **"sacrifices."** Things received may be considered: 1) in relation to the giver, and so they are called **"gifts";** 2) in relation to the receiver, and so they are called **"presents";** 3) in relation to the offerer, and so they are called **"sacrifices."** Others accommodate these three words to the Precious Blood: 1) it is a **gift**, for it was the price of our Redemption; 2) it is a **present**, for it is the only worthy oblation we can present to God; 3) it is a **sacrifice**, since it was shed for us.

The bread and wine are signed with a triple cross, to declare that the whole mystery is to be wrought by the marvelous might of the three Divine Persons.

The first prayer of the **Canon** begins with the letter **T**—not by chance, as Pope Innocent III remarks (*Lib.*

3 de myst. Miss., cap. 3), but by a special Providence, because this letter resembles the form of the Cross, whose mystery the priest should always keep before his eyes, particularly during the Canon. The letter **T** recalls to mind Ezechiel's words: "Mark 'Thau' upon the foreheads of the men that sigh and mourn . . ." (*Ezech.* 9:4).

The Memento of the Living

With hands joined, the priest prays for the living.

Be mindful, O Lord, of Thy servants and handmaids, N. and N., and of all here present, whose faith and devotion are known to Thee, for whom we offer, or who offer up to Thee, this sacrifice of praise for themselves, their families and friends, for the redemption of their souls, for the health and salvation they hope for, and who now pay tribute to Thee, the eternal, living and true God.

The second prayer of the **Canon** is the **Memento of the Living**. It is called the **Memento of the Living** because in this prayer we name only our living friends—another prayer, after the Consecration, being appointed for the remembrance of the dead. Saying the words: **"Be mindful, O Lord, of thy servants and handmaids, N. and N.,"** the priest folds his hands and makes a special remembrance of those living whom he intends to commend by a special appeal to God, that they may more abundantly participate in the fruits of the Sacrifice. Formerly, the names of all those who were to be remembered were inscribed on the diptychs. A diptych was a card folded in two like a book. The names of those who were to be specially remembered at the Mass were read from the diptych at the **Memento of the Living**. Having made a remembrance of the various intentions of the living for whom he intends to pray in particular, the priest continues with outstretched arms to pray the **Memento of the Living.**

The Communicantes

The priest prays in a low voice with extended arms.

Communicating with and honoring, in the first place, the memory of the ever glorious Virgin Mary, Mother of our Lord and God Jesus Christ; as also of the blessed Apostles and Martyrs, Peter and Paul, Andrew, James, John, Thomas, James, Philip, Bartholomew, Matthew, Simon and Thaddeus, Linus, Cletus, Clement, Sixtus, Cornelius, Cyprian, Lawrence, Chrysogonus, John and Paul, Cosmas and Damian, and of all Thy Saints, through whose merits and prayers grant that we may be always defended by the help of Thy protection, through the same Christ, our Lord. Amen.

Our prayers for all the members of the Church living on earth being ended, we naturally seek the help and intercession of those members of the same Church who now reign with God in Heaven. The Apostles' Creed teaches us to believe in the Communion of Saints. The priest therefore recites the third prayer of the **Canon** and says: **"Communicating with,"** etc.

The Lord announced to King Ezechias by the mouth of the Prophet Isaias that He would protect and save Jerusalem from the attacks of the Assyrians for His own sake and for the sake of David, His servant. The

Israelites often prayed to God to hear their supplications for the sake of Abraham, Isaac and Jacob. The Church, in like manner, appeals to the Mother of God and to the Saints, to render God more propitious to her supplications for their sakes.

In the first place we call upon the Blessed Virgin Mary, for, being the Mother of Jesus, she excels all the other Saints in dignity. To the names of the twelve Apostles we add the name of twelve martyrs who shed their blood for Christ in the early days of Christianity. Linus, Cletus and Clement were fellow laborers with St. Peter in the preaching of the Gospel at Rome. All three severally became his successors as Bishop of Rome and suffered martyrdom. Sixtus and Cornelius also sat in the Pontifical Chair and won the crown of martyrdom. Cyprian was Bishop of Carthage, and he also sealed his faith for Christ with his blood. Lawrence was deacon to Pope Sixtus II. The tortures he underwent to prove his loyalty to Christ are too well known to need repetition at this place. Chrysogonus was of a noble Roman family and was martyred at Aquileia, under Diocletian. John and Paul were brothers who, rather than worship gods of marble and brass, underwent a cruel death under Julian the Apostate. Cosmas and Damian were physicians who, for the love of God and for the welfare of their neighbor, exercised their profession gratis. They also sealed their faith with martyrdom. All these Saints except St. Cyprian are local Roman Saints. It will be seen from this prayer that the veneration of Saints was at first the veneration of martyrs.

The **Communicantes** has a small addition on the five chief feasts of the year: Christmas, the Epiphany, Easter, Ascension Day and Pentecost, referring to the mystery celebrated.

The Hanc Igitur

The priest continues to pray in a low voice, holding his hands over the oblation.

We therefore beseech Thee, O Lord, graciously to accept this oblation of our service, as also of Thy whole family, and to dispose our days in Thy peace; preserve us from eternal damnation, and rank us in the number of Thine elect, through Christ our Lord. Amen.

"Hanc igitur"—These are the Latin words with which the fourth prayer of the **Canon** begins. During the **Hanc Igitur** the priest, who joined his hands at the conclusion of the preceding prayer, **"Through the same Christ, Our Lord, Amen,"** spreads them over the offerings. The imposition of hands was introduced as a way of practically touching the sacrifice at this point, at which it is so definitely named in the prayer. In the Old Law the priest spread out his hands over the head of the victim, thus setting it apart for the altar—the victim burdened with the sins of the people and substituted in the place of sinners. This ceremony also symbolizes that Christ, Who is soon to become present under the appearances of bread and wine, is the expiatory Victim making satisfaction for our sins.

In this prayer we send to Heaven three fervent petitions: for peace on earth, deliverance from eternal punishment, and admission to eternal happiness. These favors we ask of God through Christ, Who for us was betrayed into the hands of those who hated peace; Who for us was condemned to death on the Cross; Who for us was numbered among the wicked.

With hands spread out over the oblation the priest recites the **Hanc Igitur,** that is, **"We therefore beseech Thee, O Lord,"** etc. It is customary to ring the bell at this point to remind the people of the nearness of the Consecration, so that they may await the coming of the Lord with due reverence and devotion.

The Quam Oblationem

The priest makes the Sign of the Cross five times over the offerings.

Which oblation do Thou, O God, vouchsafe in all respects to make ✠ blessed, ✠ approved, ✠ ratified, reasonable and acceptable; that it may be made for us the Body ✠ and Blood ✠ of Thy most beloved Son, Jesus Christ our Lord.

At the conclusion of the preceding prayer the priest joins his hands and then recites the prayer beginning with the words, ***"Quam oblationem,"*** that is, **"Which oblation,"** etc. This is the last prayer the priest says before the **Consecration,** and the nearer he approaches to that moment, the more interesting his words become. In the preceding prayer the priest asked Almighty God to accept the oblation. He now proceeds with the words: **"Which oblation do Thou, O God,"** etc.

We pray first that this oblation may be **blessed**, that is, that it may by the divine benediction be changed into a more noble substance; secondly, that it may be **approved**, not rejected as were (in some cases) the sacrifices of the Old Law; thirdly, that it may be **ratified**, that is, accomplished, and made a pure and spotless offering; fourthly, that it may be **reasonable**, that is, as St. Augustine explains, differing from all the sacrifices of irrational creatures, as were those of the Old Law; **acceptable** it **must** be when it becomes the Body and Blood of His well-beloved Son by the words of **Consecration.**

During the recitation of this prayer, the priest makes the Sign of the Cross five times over the offering, in remembrance of the fact that the Sacrifice now about to be consummated derives its virtue solely from the sacrifice on the Cross. Three times the Sign of the Cross is made over both species together, and then separately over the bread and the chalice. These signs give emphasis to the words of the prayer. In the first three signs we are reminded of the Blessed Trinity, from which Source the blessing of the **Consecration** is to be poured out upon the elements of bread and wine. The fivefold signing of the Cross before and after the **Consecration** also reminds us of the five wounds so conspicuous on the body of Christ.

THE CONSECRATION AND ELEVATION OF THE HOST

The priest consecrates and elevates the Sacred Host.

Who, the day before He suffered, took bread into His holy and venerable hands, and with His eyes lifted up toward Heaven, to Thee, O God, His Almighty Father, giving thanks to Thee, He blessed, broke, and gave it to His disciples, saying: Take all of you and eat of this,

FOR THIS IS MY BODY.

At the **Consecration** the priest performs the same action which Jesus Christ performed at the Last Supper. He obeys Christ's command: "Do this in commemoration of Me." He exercises the great power which was conferred upon him through the Sacrament of Holy Orders. Overcome with a sense of his utter unworthiness, it is with reverence and awe that the priest proceeds with the sublime action, saying the while: **"Who, the day before He suffered, took bread,"** etc.

At the beginning of these words the celebrant wipes his thumbs and forefingers on the corporal. He then takes the bread between the forefingers and thumbs of both hands. (These fingers are not separated again, except to touch the Blessed Sacrament, until they have been washed after the Communion. The reason for this is, lest any crumb remaining between them be lost.) He lifts up his eyes at the words, **"with His eyes lifted up toward Heaven,"** and makes a Sign of the Cross over the bread at the words **"blessed it."** Then, leaning with his elbows on the edge of the altar, he pronounces the words of Consecration: **FOR THIS IS MY BODY**. The altar breads—"hosts"—in the ciborium which are to be used for the Communion of the people are also consecrated at this time. At the words, **"Who the day before He suffered,"** etc., the ciborium is opened, and the words of **Consecration** are said over all the hosts that are to be consecrated.

The Elevation of the Host

The Catholic Church has always believed that the words of institution, **FOR THIS IS MY BODY,** are those that consecrate. Transubstantiation takes place at this moment. Immediately, therefore, follows the ceremony of the **Elevation**. The priest genuflects on one knee, still holding the Blessed Sacrament, then arises, lifts the consecrated Host up above his head to show it to the people, replaces it on the corporal and genuflects again. He adores Christ as the Angels adored Him, as the Magi falling down adored Him, as the Apostles in Galilee adored Him risen from the dead. It is impossible for a lay person to conceive the sentiments that fill the mind and heart of the priest at this solemn moment. Knowledge of his unworthiness fills his heart with fear, but faith in God's mercy fills him with hope. And thus we find the priest at the altar ministering to his Eucharistic Lord with a strange familiarity, just as we find Mary at the manger of Bethlehem lavishing upon God-made-man the tender cares of motherhood.

The Host is elevated in order to show it to the people. The people should first look upon it, and then reverently bow their heads in adoration. At each genuflection by the priest, and between them at the Elevation, the bell is rung. This is done to give notice to the people and also to arouse the attention of such as may be inattentive. The server lifts up the chasuble at the Elevation, not at the genuflection. With a modern chasuble this rubric is a mere form and a memory of the days when the vestment was more cumbersome, on account of its covering the arms. So that the priest's arms and hands might be free at the Elevation, it was necessary in olden times for the server to assist by raising the chasuble.

Before the eleventh century the **Elevation** did not take place until toward the end of the **Canon**. Before the **Pater Noster** the priest slightly elevates the Sacred Host and Chalice. This elevation is sometimes called "the Minor Elevation." The reason for introducing the **Elevation** immediately after the Consecration was the heresy of Berengarius, who died in 1088. He denied the change—**Transubstantiation**—which the Church teaches takes place at the Consecration. Besides denouncing his error in words, the Church introduced a ceremony at the celebration of Mass—the **Elevation**—which would serve as a most significant condemnation of the teaching of **Berengarius**; by holding up the consecrated species for the **adoration** of the faithful, the Church thereby declares her belief in the Real Presence of Christ under the species of bread and wine.

THE CONSECRATION AND ELEVATION OF THE CHALICE

The priest consecrates the wine and then holds up the Precious Blood for the adoration of the faithful.

In like manner, after He had supped, taking also this excellent chalice into His holy and venerable hands, and giving Thee thanks, He blessed ✠ it and gave it to His disciples, saying: Take and drink ye all of this,

FOR THIS IS THE CHALICE OF MY BLOOD, OF THE NEW AND ETERNAL TESTAMENT, THE MYSTERY OF FAITH: WHICH SHALL BE SHED FOR YOU AND FOR MANY UNTO THE REMISSION OF SINS.

As often as ye shall do these things, ye shall do them in remembrance of Me.

The **Elevation of the Host** is followed by the **Consecration of the wine**. The priest first removes the pall from the chalice. He then takes the chalice in his hands, blesses it and says: **"In like manner,"** etc.

The words, **"taking also this excellent chalice,"** mean

the chalice most excellent by reason of its contents. **"This is the Chalice of My Blood, of the New and Eternal Testament"** means, "This is My Blood, by which the New and Eternal Testament—the New Covenant—is ratified, as formerly the Old Covenant was ratified by the blood of the animal victims." He says **"Eternal Testament"** because the New Testament and the priesthood of Christ shall continue forever, nor shall any other succeed to these. **The Mystery of Faith** means that the presence of Christ in the Sacrament of the Altar is hidden from the senses and is recognized only with the "eye" of faith.

After the consecrating words have been pronounced, the priest again places the Chalice on the corporal, saying the words: **"As often as ye shall do these things, ye shall do them in remembrance of Me."** That is: As often as you do these things, namely, consecrating bread and wine, you shall do them in remembrance of My dying for you. For this reason St. Paul said: "As often as you shall eat this bread, and drink the chalice, you shall show the death of the Lord, until He come." (*1 Cor.* 11:26).

Having uttered these words, the priest genuflects before the Chalice as an act of adoration of the Precious Blood which it now contains. With both hands he then raises the Chalice on high so that the people may look upon it and adore. The Chalice is then placed again upon the corporal and covered with the pall. This being done, the priest again genuflects before it in token of his faith and adoration.

It must be noted that at the **Consecration** the priest speaks and acts not in his own name, nor in the name of the Church, nor even in the name of Christ, but he acts as Christ Himself, as though he were transformed into Christ. Therefore he leans on the edge of the altar, thereby signifying his union with Christ. What Christ did at the Last Supper, the priest does every time he celebrates the Holy Sacrifice. Nor does he say: "This is the Body of Christ," but, **"This is My Body,"** and **This is the Chalice of My Blood. . ."** just as though Christ were speaking by his mouth.

In the Mass the act of Consecration requires the exercise of Divine power. It is a miracle transcending all human and created power. God has been pleased to employ the Sacred Humanity of the Eternal Son as His instrument for the performance of this stupendous miracle, making Jesus Christ in His Sacred Humanity a sacrificing Priest until the end of time. Christ, therefore, is the Chief Priest, although He deigned to associate with Himself, as secondary priests or agents, the Apostles and their successors. Hence the words of Consecration are rightly pronounced as coming from the mouth of Christ Himself, He being the Chief Offerer, and not as coming from the mouth of the priest, who acts as Christ's official agent. Suarez says that at the moment the celebrant pronounces the words of **Consecration,** the Sacred Humanity, *by an actual and physical concurrence*, works the sublime miracle of Transubstantiation.

After the **Consecration** there is no longer bread and wine upon the altar, but the Body and Blood, Soul and Divinity of Christ; there is no longer the matter of the sacrifice which was offered a little before, but the true Victim of Calvary veiled under the species of bread and wine. The Host is separated from the Chalice because the death of the Lord is represented, in which His blood was shed and separated from His body. **Here, properly speaking, the Holy Sacrifice is accomplished.**

PRAYERS AFTER THE CONSECRATION

The priest prays in silence.

Unde et Memores

Wherefore, O Lord, we Thy servants, as also Thy holy people, calling to mind the blessed Passion of the same Christ, Thy Son Our Lord, His Resurrection from the dead and glorious Ascension into Heaven, offer unto Thy Most Excellent Majesty, of Thy gifts bestowed upon us, a pure ✠ Victim, a holy ✠ Victim, an unspotted ✠ Victim, the holy ✠ Bread of eternal life and the Chalice ✠ of everlasting salvation.

Supra Quae

Upon which vouchsafe to look with a propitious and serene countenance, and to accept them, as Thou wast graciously pleased to accept the gifts of Thy just servant Abel, and the sacrifice of our patriarch Abraham, and that which Thy high priest Melchisedech offered to Thee, a holy sacrifice, a spotless victim.

Supplices Te Rogamus

We most humbly beseech Thee, Almighty God, to command these offerings to be carried by the hands of Thy holy angel to Thy altar on high, in the sight of Thy Divine Majesty, that as many of us as, by participation at this altar, shall partake of the most sacred ✠ Body and ✠ Blood of Thy Son, may be filled with every heavenly grace and blessing, through the same Christ our Lord. Amen.

Memento

Be mindful, O Lord, of Thy servants and handmaids N. and N., who have gone before us with the sign of faith and rest in the sleep of peace. To these, O Lord, and to all who rest in Christ, grant, we beseech Thee, a place of refreshment, light and peace, through the same Christ our Lord. Amen.

The prayers which preceded the Consecration were preparations for the Sacrifice. In the prayers which follow, the virtues of the Sacrifice are applied to our wants.

Unde Et Memores

After the **Elevation of the Chalice**, with outstretched arms the priest recites the prayer beginning with the words, ***"Unde et memores,"*** that is, **"Wherefore, O Lord,"** etc.

The last words pronounced by the priest before beginning this prayer were, **"As often as ye shall do these things, ye shall do them in remembrance of Me."** In the present prayer he calls attention to the fact that what was done (at the Consecration) was done in remembrance of Christ's death. In making remembrance of Our Lord in this prayer we mention His Passion, His Resurrection and His Ascension. This is done because Christ wrought and accomplished our Redemption principally by those three means. He died to deliver us from death, He rose again to raise us to life, and He ascended into Heaven to glorify us everlastingly.

During this prayer the priest makes the Sign of the Cross five times over the Host and Chalice. These crosses are not intended as blessings over the Victim, for Christ is the source of all benediction. They are intended to signify that this is the Victim of Calvary, Who has truly suffered and Who was immolated on the Cross for man. The five crosses will recall to mind Christ's five Wounds. The first three, which are made over the Host and the Chalice together, may signify that Christ suffered, died and was buried. The last two which are made, one over the Host, and the other over the Chalice separately, remind us of the consequences of His bitter pains, namely, the separation of His soul from His body.

Supra Quae

After making the Sign of the Cross five times over the consecrated Host and the Precious Blood, with extended arms the priest commences the prayer beginning with the words ***"Supra quae"*—"Upon which"** (that is, upon the Bread of eternal life and the Chalice of everlasting salvation).

This most beautiful and impressive prayer requires a little explanation. The priest commends the Divine Victim to the Father by recalling the memory of sacrifices which He deigned to accept from the beginning of the world: those of Abel, the just man; of Abraham, the father of the faithful; and of Melchisedech, the royal priest—which, however, were only shadows of the present Sacrifice. The Church names in preference to others the sacrifices of Abel, Abraham and Melchisedech because by a more lively image they represent the sacrifice of Christ. By calling to mind these great characters at so sacred a time, the Church wishes us to cherish their virtues.

Supplices Te Rogamus

This prayer hardly needs any explanation. The attitude of the priest is now changed. Hitherto he has recited the prayers of the Canon in an erect posture, generally with his hands lifted up to Heaven. At this prayer he joins his hands before his breast and bows down his head as low as the altar will admit. In this posture of prostrate humility he recites the prayer until, toward the conclusion, kissing the altar, he resumes his former upright posture. The words of the prayer correspond with the ceremonies: **"We most humbly beseech Thee,"** etc.

By these words the priest expresses the desire that through the ministry of the Angels, who attend both upon us and upon the sacred Mysteries, the sacred Gifts now present upon the altar might be presented on the celestial altar before the eyes of the Divine Majesty. This will be done not in a physical, but moral manner, by the turning of the loving eyes of the Heavenly Father to the present Sacrifice of His Son's Body and Blood.

Before saying the words, **"by participation at this altar,"** the priest kisses the altar. This ceremony represents unto us our reconciliation with God, which was effected through the death of Christ, which is now represented upon the altar. During this prayer the celebrant again makes the Sign of the Cross over the Host and Chalice. This is done to impress upon the minds of the priest and of the people the truth that the Sacrifice which takes place upon our altars is the same as that which was once offered on Calvary. At the words, **"may be filled with every heavenly grace and blessing,"** the priest signs himself with the Cross to indicate that all graces and blessings were merited for us upon the Cross.

Memento of the Dead

Through this Sacrifice, which the priest rightly supposes to have been received favorably by God, he asks, moreover, for eternal rest for the faithful departed, that is, the Church Suffering in Purgatory. He prays for the dead in these words: **"Be mindful, O Lord, of Thy servants and handmaids,"** etc.

At the **Memento of the Dead** the priest joins his hands before his breast; in the meantime, he mentions the names of persons for whom he particularly wishes to pray or offer up the Mass. Then he extends his hands to pray for all who are detained in Purgatory, saying: **"To these, O Lord,"** etc.

This is done in order, as St. Augustine remarks, "that such religious duty, whenever it is neglected by parents, children, relatives or friends, may be supplied by our common Mother, the Church."

The Nobis Quoque Peccatoribus

The priest strikes his breast.

And to us sinners also, Thy servants, hoping in the multitude of Thy mercies, deign to grant some part and fellowship with Thy holy Apostles and Martyrs; with John, Stephen, Matthias, Barnabas, Ignatius, Alexander, Marcellinus, Peter, Felicitas, Perpetua, Agatha, Lucy, Agnes, Cecilia, Anastasia, and with all Thy Saints; into whose company we beseech Thee to admit us, not weighing our mer-

its, but freely pardoning our offenses, through Christ our Lord.

Per Quem and Minor Elevation

Through Whom, O Lord, Thou dost always create, ✠ sanctify, ✠ quicken, ✠ bless and give us all these good things.

Through ✠ Him, and with ✠ Him, and in ✠ Him, is to Thee, ✠ O God the Father Almighty, ✠ in the unity of the Holy Ghost, all honor and glory.

P. World without end.

S. Amen.

The Nobis Quoque Peccatoribus

Having finished our prayer for the faithful departed in Purgatory, who, though they were sinners, are yet eternally secured in the grace of God, which they can never lose, we again turn our thoughts upon ourselves, who are sinners of a very different kind—not knowing whether we possess the grace of God, and if we do, uncertain whether we shall persevere to the end in that grace. The priest says aloud the first words, ***"Nobis quoque peccatoribus"*—"And to us sinners also,"** in order that he may be better heard in this humble acknowledgment. He also strikes his breast, in imitation of the publican in the Gospel, as he says: **"And to us sinners,"** etc.

Through this prayer the priest, as it were, opens and contemplates the heavenly court of the Church Triumphant, which, although we are sinners, is prepared for us by the blood of this divine Host, Christ Jesus.

Among the Saints mentioned in this prayer, St. John the Baptist is named first, and rightly so, for it was of him that Christ said: "There hath not risen among them that are born of women a greater than John the Baptist." (*Matt.* 11:11). St. Stephen was the very first to suffer martyrdom for Christ. St. Matthias was divinely elected by lot into the Apostleship, to supply the sacred number of twelve, which had been diminished by the traitorous conduct of Judas. St. Barnabas was a native of Cyprus and one of the seventy-two disciples of Jesus Christ; he was a companion of St. Paul and was put to death during the reign of Nero. St. Ignatius (of Antioch) was a disciple of St. John the Apostle and the second successor of St. Peter in the bishopric of Antioch; he suffered martyrdom under the Emperor Trajan. St. Alexander was the sixth Pope. Having ruled the Church for ten years, he was martyred together with his deacons Eventius and Theodulous under the Emperor Adrian. St. Marcellinus was a priest of the Church of Rome during the reign of Diocletian. He baptized Paulina, the daughter of Artemiras, keeper of the prison of the city—whom St. Peter the exorcist had delivered of a malignant spirit that possessed her—together with her relatives who witnessed the miracle. For this he was most strangely tormented, and in the end beheaded by order of the Judge Serenus, who could not induce him to renounce his Faith. The St. Peter mentioned in this prayer was ordained an exorcist. He suffered martyrdom for assisting at the Baptism of Paulina administered by St. Marcellinus.

St. Perpetua was a noble Roman lady who died the death of a martyr in Carthage under the Emperor Severus around the year 203. Martyred with her was the slave girl St. Felicitas, who had given birth in prison.

Both saints had received Baptism not long before their death. St. Agatha was famed for her virtue and beauty. She spurned the proposals of Quintianus, Governor of Sicily, whereupon his disordered affection was changed to devilish hatred and extreme desire to revenge himself. After many insupportable torments she was martyred, having first both her breasts cut off by order of Quintianus. St. Lucy, having by her prayers at the sepulchre of St. Agatha obtained from God the cure of her invalid mother, vowed to distribute to the poor all her possessions, whereupon he to whom she was betrothed accused her of being a Christian. She was subjected to the most horrible torments. St. Agnes was beheaded in 317 on account of her steadfastness in virtue and in faith. St. Cecilia was another famous martyr in the early Church. She suffered martyrdom by being beheaded together with her husband, Valerian, whom she married against her wishes and whom she afterward converted to the Catholic Faith. St. Anastasia was a very charitable Roman lady. On account of her great charity and faith, she incurred the displeasure of her husband Publius. Not being able to divert her from the Faith, he caused her to be burned alive.

Mention is made of these Saints in particular because their names shone forth so prominently in early ecclesiastical history. The antiquity of this prayer bears witness to the antiquity of the practice of invoking the Saints. At the conclusion of this prayer, the priest again joins his hands. By this ceremony, which is used here at the commemoration of the Saints, we are reminded that through the merits of Christ, Who is our Head, we hope to be united with Him and His Saints in everlasting glory.

Per Quem and Minor Elevation

The following prayer may be regarded as the continuation of the preceding. The priest now prays: **"Through Whom,"** etc.

The meaning of this prayer is that through Christ, all the blessings necessary for our temporal life, which are represented by the bread and wine, God always **creates**, or causes to spring forth from the earth for us; He **sanctifies** them, by accepting the bread and wine which were offered to Him as the matter of the sacrifice; He **quickens** (gives life to) this matter by the words of Consecration, changing it into the Body and Blood of Christ; He **blesses** it, inasmuch as this Sacrament is the fountain of every grace and blessing; and in Communion He **gives** us all that the soul desires.

When saying the words, **"sanctify", "quicken"** and **"bless,"** the priest makes the Sign of the Cross with his hand three times over the Host and the Chalice. This is done to indicate that all things are sanctified, quickened and blessed through the Cross of our Redeemer. Before saying the words: **"Through Him,"** etc., the priest removes the pall from the Chalice, genuflects as an act of adoration, and holding the Host in his right hand and the Chalice in his left, he makes with the sacred Host three crosses over the Chalice at the words: **"Through Him, and with Him, and in Him."** The words and ceremony indicate that the highest honor which is rendered to God **through, with** and **in** Christ flows from His blood-shedding on the Cross, now mystically represented upon the altar. When mentioning God the Father and the Holy Ghost, the Sign of the Cross is made twice, with the Sacred Host between the Chalice and the priest's breast.

The Sign of the Cross is made three times in the first instance because Christ is mentioned three times: **"Through Him, and with Him, and in Him."** And in these instances the Sign of the Cross is made over the Chalice because it contains the Blood of Christ. In the second instance, the Sign of the Cross is made once when mentioning the Father, and once when mentioning the Holy Ghost. In this instance the Sign of the Cross is made outside of the Chalice which contains the Blood of Christ.

When saying the words, **"sanctify," "quicken"** and **"bless,"** the priest makes the Sign of the Cross, but he does not at the word ***"creas"*—"create."** Alexander of Hales gives this explanation: The Sign of the Cross is a representation of Our Lord's Passion. Because the creation of man was no cause of His Passion, but the *fall* of man was thereby to be repaired, therefore the Sign of the Cross is made when sanctification, vivification and benediction, the fruits of the Passion, are mentioned, but not when creation is mentioned. St. Thomas says that this is done because man did not have by nature, in his creation, that which he has since obtained by the Cross of Christ in his Redemption.

In saying the last words of this prayer, **"all honor and glory,"** the priest elevates a little both the Host and the Chalice. Up to the eleventh century, the Body and Blood of Christ were here held up at this point in the Mass to receive the adoration of the faithful. But, as has been already observed, about the year 1047 a more solemn elevation was adopted by the Church to furnish a public profession of her ancient faith concerning the Real Presence, in contradiction to the heretical teachings of Berengarius. The elevation at this part of the Mass is called the "Minor Elevation" or "Second Elevation" or "Little Elevation" to distinguish it from the Elevation which follows the Consecration.

Chapter 4

The Communion, The Third of the Three Principal Parts of the Mass

The Completion of the Sacrifice by the Priest's Partaking of the Sacrificial Food

This part of the Mass consists of the preparation for Communion, Communion itself, and the prayers after Communion.

The Pater Noster (Our Father)

The priest prays aloud with arms extended.

P. Forever and ever. *(Per omnia saecula saeculorum.)*
S. Amen.

P. Let us pray. *(Oremus.)* Instructed by Thy saving precepts, and following Thy divine instruction, we dare to say:

Our Father, Who art in Heaven, hallowed be Thy name; Thy kingdom come; Thy will be done on earth as it is in Heaven. Give us this day our daily bread; and forgive us our trespasses, as we forgive those who trespass against us, and lead us not into temptation,

S. But deliver us from evil.
P. Amen.

The priest, having performed the Minor Elevation, places the Host upon the corporal, covers the Chalice with the pall and genuflects. He then says in a loud voice, ***"Per omnia saecula saeculorum"*—"forever and ever."** These words, as is evident, belong to the preceding prayer; they express the yearning of the pious soul that honor and glory be rendered to the three Divine Persons forever and ever. The people, through the mouth of the altar boy, answer: **"Amen,"** thus confirming and ratifying all that the priest prayed for in secret.

The preceding prayer, **Per Quem (**with the **Minor Elevation)**, concluded the **Canon**. Hence the priest now breaks the silence he has observed since the **Sanctus** by saying aloud, ***"Oremus"*—"Let us pray."**

Before beginning the **Our Father**, the Lord's Prayer, the priest reminds the faithful that it is out of obedience to the will of Christ that we say the **Our Father**. In the eleventh chapter of St. Luke we read: "And it came to pass, that as He was in a certain place praying, when He ceased, one of His disciples said to Him: Lord, teach us to pray . . . And He said to them: When you pray, say: Our Father, etc." (Cf. *Luke* 11:1-2).

Hence before beginning the **Our Father**, immediately after saying ***"Oremus,"*** the priest prays: **"Instructed by Thy saving precepts, and following Thy divine instruction, we dare to say: Our Father,"** etc.

During the **Canon,** the priest extended no invitation to the congregation to join him in prayer. During that time he is supposed to have entered into the Holy of Holies and to be engaged in earnest prayer alone, separated, as it were, from the people for a time. But at the ***Pater Noster*—Our Father,** which now follows, the priest raises his voice and recites aloud, with extended arms, the seven petitions of the **Our Father.**

Here the **Communion** is considered to begin. The Lord's Prayer is a preparation for it. Communion is not only the complement of the Sacrifice, but also a family banquet at which the children of God, around the paternal board, feast with their most loving Father; wherefore, at the Our Father they begin to greet Him and to excite in their souls filial affections and to express them, saying, **"Our Father . . . give us this day our daily bread."** To show that the people are united with the priest in the recitation of this prayer, they themselves utter the words of the last petition, by the voice of the server: ***"Sed libera nos a malo"*—"But deliver us from evil."** To this the priest says, ***"Amen,"*** a response which is expressive of confidence that God will hear their prayer.

The Libera Nos

The priest, making the Sign of the Cross with the paten over himself, prays at the center of the altar.

Deliver us, we beseech Thee, O Lord, from all evils, past, present and to come; and by the intercession of the blessed and glorious Mary ever Virgin, Mother of God, and of the holy Apostles, Peter and Paul, and Andrew, and of all the Saints, mercifully grant peace in our days, that through the assistance of Thy mercy we may be always free from sin, and secure from all disturbance. Through the same Jesus Christ, Thy Son our Lord, Who liveth and reigneth with Thee, in the unity of the Holy Ghost, God, forever and ever. Amen.

In reciting the **Pater Noster** the priest dwells particularly on the last petition, **"Deliver us from evil,"** by immediately reciting another prayer beginning with the words, ***"Libera nos,"*** etc.—**"Deliver us, we beseech Thee,"** etc.

When the priest begins this prayer, he draws forth the paten from beneath the corporal, where it was placed after the offering of the bread. When saying the words, **"grant peace in our days,"** etc., he makes on himself the Sign of the Cross with the paten and then kisses it reverently as the instrument of peace; for the Sacred Host, the peace of Christians, is about to be deposited upon it. The Sign of the Cross is made at this point to indicate that it was by the Cross that Christ became "our peace" by the shedding of His blood upon the Cross. (Cf. *Eph*. 2:14). After kissing the paten, the priest places upon it the Sacred Host, which heretofore rested upon the corporal. The paten with the Sacred Host resting upon it is then placed to the right of the Chalice, to indicate that blood and water issued forth from the opened side of our Redeemer.

That special mention should be made of St. Andrew in this prayer must naturally arrest the attention of the devout soul. We can readily understand why the Mother of Jesus and the princes of the Apostles should be specially mentioned. St. Andrew was a great favorite with the early Christians at Rome because he was the brother of St. Peter. Hence his name was mentioned together with that of his brother, St. Peter. The medieval theologian Gabriel Biel says that, to obtain the gift of peace, St. Andrew is mentioned because his martyrdom resembled very much the Passion of Christ, in virtue whereof, peace is given unto us.

The Breaking of the Host

The priest breaks the Host and lets a small Particle drop into the Chalice.

P. Forever and ever. ***(Per omnia saecula saeculorum.)***
S. Amen. ***(Amen.)***

P. The peace ✠ of the Lord be ✠ always with ✠ you. ***(Pax Domini sit semper vobiscum.)***
S. And with thy spirit. ***(Et cum spiritu tuo.)***
P. May this mingling and consecration of the Body and Blood of our Lord Jesus Christ avail us who receive it unto everlasting life. Amen.

Having arrived at the words, **"Through the same Jesus Christ,"** etc., the concluding words of the prayer **Libera Nos,** the priest genuflects to adore the Blessed Sacrament, then, taking the Sacred Host and holding it over the Chalice, he divides it into three parts. In this ceremony he imitates our Divine Saviour, Who broke the Consecrated **"Bread,"** now His Body, before giving it to His Apostles. When the sacred Host is divided, the Body of Christ is not broken. The appearances of bread are divided, but the Body of Christ itself is present in each part entire and living, in a true though mysterious manner.

At the breaking of the Host, the priest holds it over the Chalice, reciting at the same time the concluding words of the **Libera Nos.** At the words, **"Through the same Jesus Christ, Thy Son, our Lord,"** he divides the Host into two halves, holding it over the Chalice. The half which was held in the right hand is then placed upon the paten. Saying the words: **"Who liveth and reigneth with Thee,"** the celebrant breaks a small

Particle off the other half, which he holds in his left hand. Upon arriving at the words, **"in the unity of the Holy Ghost,"** he places the half which he was holding in his left hand beside the other upon the paten. At the last words: ***"Per omnia saecula saeculorum"*—"for ever and ever,"** the priest raises his voice; the server answers: **"Amen."** He then says aloud: ***"Pax ✠ Domini sit ✠ semper vobis ✠ cum*—"The peace of the Lord be always with you."** While saying these words he makes the Sign of the Cross three times over the Chalice with the small Particle broken off the one half of the Sacred Host. The server having answered, **"And with thy spirit,"** the little Particle is dropped into the Chalice. The priest then says: **"May this mingling and consecration of the Body and Blood of our Lord Jesus Christ avail us who receive it unto everlasting life. Amen."** This prayer having been recited, the Chalice is covered again with the pall and the priest bends his knee in humble adoration.

Why a Particle Is Dropped into the Chalice

The breaking of the Host is a figure of the death of Christ, by which His humanity seemingly was broken. It is also a preparation for the great banquet. This preparation for worthily disposing the hearts of the communicants consists in peace and in union, in charity and concord with God and between ourselves. This Peace **of the Lord,** Christ merited for us on the Cross, and we should preserve it through the cross. The Host is broken over the Chalice to indicate that the Precious Blood flowed from the bruised body of Christ.

A small Particle of the consecrated Host is mingled with the Precious Blood to show that our Lord's Body is not without His Blood, nor His Blood without His Body. The separated appearances of bread and wine might lead one to believe that the Body and Blood of Christ are also separated. The mingling of the two species dispels the illusion, reminding us that under each appearance, the one, living Victim of the Cross is present. This ceremony also recalls to mind the union of the divinity with the humanity in the Incarnation.

The Agnus Dei

Striking his breast three times, the priest says the Agnus Dei.

Lamb of God, Who takest away the sins of the world, have mercy on us.
Lamb of God, Who takest away the sins of the world, have mercy on us.
Lamb of God, Who takest away the sins of the world, grant us peace.

The **Agnus Dei** occurs toward the end of the **Canon**, following the prayer, **"May this mingling,"** etc. Having finished saying this prayer, the priest covers the Chalice with the pall, genuflects, rises, inclines his head profoundly toward the altar and with a loud voice says: ***"Agnus Dei, qui tollis peccata mundi, miserere nobis"—*** **"Lamb of God, Who takest away the sins of the world, have mercy on us."** He repeats this formula two more times, the third time substituting ***"dona nobis pacem"—*** **"grant us peace,"** for ***"miserere nobis"—*****"have mercy on us."** By this threefold recitation of the same prayer the Church wishes to teach us how ardently we should desire, and how fervently we should pray for the peace of the Lord, that is, for full remission of all our sins and all punishment due to them. While saying the ***Agnus Dei*** the priest strikes his breast three times in testimony of his sorrow and compunction.

In Requiem Masses the **Agnus Dei** is changed somewhat. ***"Dona eis requiem"*****—"grant them rest"** is substituted for ***miserere nobis;*** and ***"dona eis requiem sempiternam"*****—"grant them eternal rest"** for **dona nobis pacem.** In this case the priest does not strike his breast, as he is not praying for himself.

Christ Is The Lamb of God

Christ is called the "Lamb of God" or the *"Agnus Dei."* Though the Prophet Isaias, long before Christ's coming into the world, compared Our Lord to a lamb, St. John the Baptist was the first actually to bestow this name upon Him. "Behold the Lamb of God" was the exclamation of St. John when he pointed out our Saviour to the unbelieving multitudes. When the devout worshiper assists at Mass, the recital of the **Agnus Dei** will recall to mind such instances in the Old Testament as the Paschal Lamb of the Jews, "without blemish," whose blood, sprinkled on the doorposts, saved from the Destroying Angel—a figure of the Immaculate Lamb, whose blood saved from eternal death. The **Agnus Dei** also reminds him of the perpetual offering of a lamb, morning and night, in the Temple—a figure of the perpetual Sacrifice of the altar in the New Testament. From St. John the Baptist, St. John the Evangelist caught the fullness of the symbolism of the "lamb" and repeated it in the fourth and fifth chapters of *Revelations* (the *Apocalypse*) in such a way as to foreshadow the pomp of the Solemn Mass: the Lamb upon the altar as upon a throne; the attendant clergy as four-and-twenty ancients seated, clothed in white vestments; the chanting of the *"Sanctus, sanctus, sanctus";* the incense arising from the golden censers, and the music of harps; and then, as by a sudden change in the midst of all, "a Lamb standing as it were **slain.**" (*Apoc.* 5:6). Such thoughts flood the mind of the priest as he bends low before the Sacred Host and repeats the words, ***"Agnus Dei,"*** etc.

The Three Communion Prayers

Bowing low before the altar, the priest recites the three Communion prayers.

O Lord Jesus Christ, Who didst say to Thine Apostles: "Peace I leave with you, My peace I give to you," regard not my sins but the faith of Thy Church; and be pleased to grant her peace and unity according to Thy will; Who livest and reignest, God, forever and ever. Amen.

O Lord Jesus Christ, Son of the living God, Who, according to the will of the Father, through the cooperation of the Holy Ghost, hast by Thy death given life to the world, deliver me by this Thy most sacred Body and Blood from all my iniquities and from all evils; and make me always adhere to Thy commandments, and never permit me to be separated from Thee; Who livest and reignest with the same God the Father and the Holy Ghost, God, forever and ever. Amen.

Let not the reception of Thy Body, O Lord Jesus

Christ, which I, though unworthy, presume to receive, be to my judgment and condemnation; but through Thy mercy may it be unto me a safeguard and remedy both for soul and body; Who with God the Father, in the unity of the Holy Ghost, livest and reignest, God, forever and ever. Amen.

The First Communion Prayer

Maintaining the same attitude, the priest continues the same request for peace in another prayer which begins with the words, ***"Domine Jesu Christe"*—"O Lord Jesus Christ,"** etc.

It will be noted from the wording of this prayer that it is a humble petition for the blessing of peace for the Church. But as the peace of God cannot be enjoyed unless we live also in peace with our fellow men, the custom arose in the Church of saluting one another with a holy kiss of peace during the recital of this prayer: "Salute one another with a holy kiss." (*Rom.* 16:16). The celebrant would give the deacon the salutation of peace, who then would proclaim solemnly to the people that they should salute one another with the kiss of peace. We have a remnant of this old custom preserved in the ceremonies of a Solemn Mass, when the priest, after the above prayer for peace, gives the salutation of peace to the deacon, saying, **"Peace be with you,"** and the deacon answering, **"And with thy spirit."** The deacon then in the same manner salutes the sub-deacon.

In the thirteenth century a substitute for the actual kiss was introduced in the shape of a small wooden tablet or metal plate bearing a pious representation, usually of the crucifixion. This tablet was called "Pax" (meaning "peace"). It was kissed by the celebrant and was then carried to others to be likewise kissed by them. This ceremony reminded the faithful that they should be ready to forgive all injuries and not entertain any unchristian enmities, especially if they were about to receive Holy Communion.

The Second Communion Prayer

The two prayers which follow are recited as an immediate preparation for Holy Communion. The happy moment in which priest and people will be united with their Lord is near at hand. "And the work is great, for a house is prepared not for man, but for God." (*1 Par.* 29:1). Therefore, with bowed head and eyes fixed upon the Sacred Host lying before him upon the altar, the priest continues to pray: **"O Lord Jesus Christ,"** etc.

St. Peter once made the solemn profession of faith to Our Lord: "Thou art Christ, the Son of the living God." (*Matt.* 16:16). He beheld only Christ's humanity, yet he acknowledged His divinity. Upon the altar, Christ's humanity and divinity are concealed under the appearances of bread and wine, and yet the priest professes both with the liveliest faith at the moment he is about to receive the Eucharist, saying: **"O Lord Jesus Christ, Son of the Living God."** He also makes profession of his faith in the redeeming Blood of Christ, entreating Him to apply the fruits thereof to his sinful soul, saying: **"Deliver me by this Thy most sacred Body and Blood from all my iniquities,"** etc.

The text of this prayer reminds us that the work of the Redemption was accomplished by Christ **"according to the will of the Father"** and **"through the cooperation of the Holy Ghost."** The Father did not spare His only begotten Son. The Son, out of love for the

Father, agreed upon the plan of Redemption, "becoming obedient unto death, even to the death of the cross." (*Phil.* 2:8). The Holy Ghost cooperated in this work, for "by the Holy Ghost" Christ "offered Himself unspotted unto God." (*Heb.* 9:14). This prayer reminds us that we should approach Holy Communion professing our faith, "For as often as you shall eat this bread, and drink the chalice, you shall show the death of the Lord." (*1 Cor.* 11:26). It reminds us that we should not lose sight of our unworthiness: "Let a man prove himself." (*1 Cor.* 11:28).

The Third Communion Prayer

This third prayer refers directly to the reception of Communion. The priest first expresses his unworthiness to receive, then also his fear lest he communicate unworthily, saying: **"Let not the reception,"** etc.

At this solemn moment the priest remembers well the words of the Apostle: "Let a man prove himself: and so let him eat of that bread, and drink of the chalice." (*1 Cor.* 11:28). This unworthiness of which the priest makes mention does not refer to mortal sin, for to communicate in this state would be sacrilegious, but it refers to the many imperfections and frailties to which poor human nature is heir. Mistrusting himself on account of his repeated falls, the priest prays that the reception of the Sacrament "may not be to his condemnation"; but, full of confidence in Him Who has said, "If any man eat of this bread, he shall live for ever," he expresses his hope that the reception of the Eucharist will be a "safeguard and remedy both for soul and body."

THE COMMUNION OF THE PRIEST

Taking the Sacred Host in his hands, the priest says:

I will take the Bread of Heaven, and call upon the Name of the Lord.

Domine, Non Sum Dignus

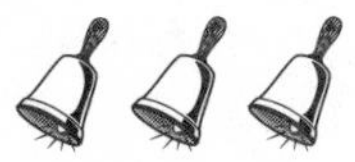

Striking his breast with humility, he says three times:

Lord, I am not worthy that Thou shouldst enter under my roof; but only say the word, and my soul shall be healed.

The three Communion prayers were recited by the priest with head bowed and eyes fixed upon the Sacred Host resting upon the paten. These prayers being ended, he genuflects in token of adoration and, rising, takes the Sacred Host in his hands, saying: **"I will take the Bread of Heaven, and call upon the Name of the Lord."** The Eucharist is here called the **"Bread of Heaven"** in allusion to the manna given to the Israelites in the desert, which was a figure of the Eucharist. Being about to perform the sublimest act in religion, to partake of the Body and Blood of Christ, what can we do better than call upon the Name of the Lord? "I met with trouble and sorrow: and I called upon the name of the Lord." (*Ps*. 114:3-4).

Domine, Non Sum Dignus

With trembling hand, but at the same time with great confidence in the invocation of the Name of the Lord, the priest takes the Sacred Host in his left hand, holding the paten beneath it with the same hand. He then reverently bows his head and, with eyes fixed upon the Sacred Host, with his right hand strikes his breast three times, repeating the words of the centurion: ***"Domine, non sum dignus . . ."*—"Lord, I am not worthy that Thou shouldst enter under my roof; but only say the word, and my soul shall be healed."** This prayer is recited three times, and the bell is sounded each time to excite the attention of all those present to this important part of the Mass. These words of the centurion—expressive of the greatest humility and confidence and so much praised by Christ Himself—the Church puts in the mouth of her children whenever they are about to receive Holy Communion. Our faith in the Real Presence of Our Lord in the Eucharist informs us of the greatness of this Sacrament. Our knowledge of our own sinfulness and frailty informs us of our unworthiness to receive the Sacrament. This faith and this knowledge engender in the soul fear, which is expressed in the words: **"Lord, I am not worthy."** But this fear is soon dispelled by a recollection of the Saviour's goodness and kindness, as His words again resound in our soul: "Come to me, all you that labor and are burdened, and I will refresh you." (*Matt.* 11:28). Buoyed up with hope and confidence, we repeat: **"Only say the word, and my soul shall be healed."**

The author of *The Imitation of Christ* says beautifully: "When I consider Thy greatness, O Lord, and my own vileness, I tremble exceedingly, and am confounded in myself. For if I come not, I fly from life, and if I intrude unworthily, I incur Thy displeasure. What then shall I do?"

The priest prays:

May the Body of our Lord Jesus Christ preserve my soul unto life everlasting. Amen.

The priest reverently consumes the Sacred Host.

After receiving, the priest pauses for a brief meditation, then says:

What return shall I make to the Lord for all He has given me? I will take the chalice of salvation and call upon the Name of the Lord. Praising, I will call upon the Lord, and I shall be saved from my enemies.

Making the Sign of the Cross with the Chalice, the priest says:

May the Blood of our Lord Jesus Christ preserve my soul unto life everlasting. Amen.

The priest reverently consumes the Precious Blood.

We are reminded of the words of *The Apocalypse:* "Let us be glad and rejoice . . . for the marriage of the Lamb is come, and His bride [the soul] hath prepared herself. . . . Blessed are they that are called to the marriage supper of the Lamb." (*Apoc.* 19:7-9).

Before receiving the Sacred Host, the priest makes with it the Sign of the Cross over himself, to express in a lively manner that the Sacred Body which he is about to receive is the same Body that was crucified for us upon the Cross on Calvary. While performing this ceremony, he says: **"May the Body of our Lord Jesus Christ preserve my soul unto life everlasting. Amen."** Thereupon the priest, after the manner of the Apostles at the Last Supper, eats that same celestial

Bread of the immolated Body of the Lord. As the bread ministered by the Angel to the Prophet Elias so fortified him as to enable him to walk to the mountain of God, Horeb; and as the bread which fell from Heaven brought the people of Israel through the desert into the Land of Promise, even so the priest prays that this heavenly Bread may be his true Viaticum (food for the journey) leading safely through the desert of this world to that land of joys promised to God's elect.

After the priest has received the Sacred Host he pauses for a little while to meditate upon the great mystery. With eyes cast down and hands reverently folded upon his breast, wrapped in earnest thought, the words of St. Augustine may come to his mind: "Thou hast created us for Thyself, O Lord, and our hearts are restless until they rest in Thee."

After this brief meditation the priest removes the pall from the Chalice and genuflects as a token of adoration to the Precious Blood. Any small Particles of the Sacred Host that may have fallen upon the corporal are gathered together by scraping the paten over the corporal. These small Particles gathered upon the paten are then brushed from the paten into the Chalice. Out of respect for the Blessed Eucharist, the Church requires that her ministers use great precaution so that none of the sacred Particles may be lost.

As the priest meditates earnestly upon the wondrous gift received in Holy Communion, he is overcome with astonishment and exclaims, ***"Quid retribuam . . ."*—** **"What return shall I make to the Lord for all He has given me?"** In Holy Communion the infinite God, in His infinite love, grants an infinite gift. All-powerful though He be, He cannot give more; all-wise though He be, He knows not what more to give; all-bountiful though

He be, He has not more to give. In answer to the question, "What return shall I make to the Lord?" the priest finds that he can only give what has been given. He therefore takes the Chalice with his right hand and says, **"I will take the chalice of salvation,"** etc.

God has no need of our goods. (Cf. *Ps.* 15:2). To His kind and loving heart it is sufficient thanks if we gratefully receive and rightly use His gifts.

Having uttered this exultant prayer, the priest takes the Chalice in his right hand and makes with it the Sign of the Cross over himself to indicate again that it is from the Cross on Calvary that the redeeming grace of Christ's blood flows upon us. As he does this, he says, **"May the Blood of our Lord Jesus Christ preserve my soul unto life everlasting. Amen."** He then reverently consumes the Precious Blood, holding the paten beneath the Chalice so that no drop of the sacred species may be spilled.

The priest who celebrates Mass receives both species (that is, he receives Communion under the form of bread and under the form of wine) because he must consume the Sacrifice, which was offered up under two species. At the Last Supper, when Christ commissioned His Apostles to do as He had done, He said to them: "Drink ye all of this." No one, however, was present but the Apostles, all of whom had been ordained sacrificing priests. The priest or bishop or even the pope who receives Holy Communion without saying Mass, receives Communion under one species only, like any layman.

Communion of the Faithful

If Communion is to be distributed to the faithful, the distribution takes place now. The server says the Confiteor (as on p. 90, substituting the word "Father" for "brethren"), and the priest responds:*

P. May Almighty God have mercy upon you, forgive you your sins and bring you to everlasting life.

S. Amen.

P. May the Almighty and merciful Lord grant us pardon, absolution and remission of our sins.

S. Amen.

Holding up a Host, the priest says:

Behold the Lamb of God *(Ecce Agnus Dei)*, behold Him Who taketh away the sins of the world.

The priest says three times, and the people strike their breasts in humility each time:

Lord, I am not worthy *(Domine, non sum dignus)* that Thou shouldst enter under my roof; but only say the word, and my soul shall be healed.

The communicants now move to the Communion rail and kneel. The server holds a Communion paten under the chin of each one in turn, and the priest says to each communicant, placing a sacred Host on his tongue:

May the Body of Our Lord Jesus Christ preserve thy soul unto life everlasting. Amen.

---

* To receive Holy Communion *worthily,* one must be a Catholic, in the state of grace (that is, free from unconfessed mortal sin), and have fasted from food and drink (except water and medicine) for an hour before receiving. (Fasting voluntarily for a longer period, as was formerly required—e.g., from midnight or for 3 hours—is very praiseworthy.)

Each communicant reverently returns to his seat and spends some time in silent prayer to Our Lord, Who is now sacramentally present within him. This is a most precious time in which to make acts of thanksgiving, love, adoration and petition, either in one's own words or reading from a prayer book. It is highly recommended that the communicant remain in church for approximately 15 minutes after the time of receiving, since the sacred species remain within one's body for approximately this length of time. The Body of Christ is present as long as the appearances of bread remain.

If one is not going to receive Communion, one should make a *Spiritual Communion.* A Spiritual Communion consists of interior acts of love for Our Lord and of desire to receive Him.*

THE ABLUTIONS

The priest purifies the chalice and covers it with the veil.

The First Ablution

Grant, O Lord, that what we have taken with our mouth, we may receive with a pure mind; and from a temporal gift may it become for us an eternal remedy.

---

* A Spiritual Communion may be made using these words:

My Jesus, I believe that Thou art in the Blessed Sacrament. I love Thee above all things, and I long for Thee in my soul. Since I cannot now receive Thee sacramentally, come at least spiritually into my heart. As though Thou hast already come, I embrace Thee and unite myself entirely to Thee; never permit me to be separated from Thee.

The Second Ablution

May Thy Body, O Lord, which I have received, and Thy Blood which I have drunk, cleave to my inmost parts; and grant that no stain of sin may remain in me, whom this pure and holy Sacrament has refreshed, Who livest and reignest for ever and ever. Amen.

As soon as the priest has consumed the Precious Blood, all the essential parts of the Mass are completed. After the Hosts have all been consumed or placed in the tabernacle, the Victim has now disappeared from our altar. The Sacrifice is now accomplished. What follows are prayers of thanksgiving and the ablutions or purifying of the sacred vessels that have been used for such solemn purposes.

The First Ablution

Immediately after receiving the sacred Blood the priest holds out the chalice to the server who pours in a little wine from the cruet. During this act the priest recites the prayer: ***"Quod ore sumpsimus"*****—"Grant, O Lord, that what we have taken with our mouth,"** etc. In this prayer we ask God for a twofold benefit: first, that our actual Communion may also be spiritual, that is, productive of grace in our souls; and secondly, we ask that our partaking of this Sacrament in this life may bring about our eternal happiness in the next.

The Second Ablution

After drinking the wine which was poured into the chalice for the first ablution, the priest takes the chalice in both hands and, holding the two forefingers and thumbs over the chalice, walks to the Epistle side of the altar. A little wine and water are poured over the priest's forefingers and thumbs into the chalice as a second ablution. During this ceremony the priest prays: ***"Corpus tuum, Domine, quod sumpsi"*—"May Thy Body, O Lord,"** etc.

In this prayer we ask that we may experience the efficacy of this Sacrament. By the "inmost parts" of the soul (Latin: *viscera*) we are to understand her powers, such as understanding, free will and memory.* And here we ask that to these powers of our soul this precious Food may so adhere so as not to pass quickly through our minds, as some bodily foods pass though the stomach without giving any nourishment or strength.

The Reasons for the Ablutions

These two ablutions after Communion are performed out of respect for the Holy Eucharist. The wine and water are poured into the chalice for the purpose of consuming completely any remains of the sacramental species. The priest washes the tips of his forefingers and thumbs over the chalice at the last ablution so that none of the sacred Particles may adhere to his fingers. It is with these fingers that he handles the Sacred Host during the Mass. It would be most unbecoming that the hands which have touched that incorruptible Body should touch a corruptible body before they were first diligently washed. From the time of the Consecration up to the second ablution, the priest

* "*Viscera*—in the first place means *entrails* (in Holy Scripture often regarded as the seat of the affections), then the *interior,* the inmost part of the heart." —Rev. Dr. Nicholas Gihr, *The Holy Sacrifice of the Mass* (St. Louis: B. Herder, 1943), p. 747, note 2.

always holds his hands in such a manner that the tips of the forefingers and thumbs are joined. This is done so that nothing may be touched by those members with which the priest is obliged to handle the Holy Eucharist.

After the priest has purified his fingers he returns to the center, placing the chalice upon the altar. He then takes the purificator and dries his fingers. This being done, he consumes the water and wine which were poured into the chalice at the last ablution. The chalice is wiped dry with the purificator. The purificator, paten and pall are now again placed upon the chalice. The corporal is folded and inserted in the burse. The chalice is then covered with the veil, and the burse is again placed upon it.

Transferring the Missal

While the priest purifies the chalice, the server carries the Missal from the Gospel side (the left) to the Epistle side. It must be remembered that at the beginning of the Mass the Missal was on the Epistle side.

By the transferal of the Missal again to the Epistle side after the Communion, we are reminded of the final conversion of the Jewish race. Hugo of St. Victor says: "The priest returns to the right of the altar to signify that at the end of the world Christ shall return to the Jews, whom now He has rejected until the fullness of the Gentiles be admitted, for then the remainder of Israel, according to the Scriptures, shall be saved." St. Paul speaks of the conversion of the Jews to Christianity when he says: "Blindness in part has happened in Israel, until the fullness of the Gentiles should come in." (*Rom.* 11:25).

The Communion Antiphon

The priest reads the Communion Antiphon.

We bless the God of heaven, and we will praise Him in the sight of all the living, because He hath shown His mercy to us. (Communion antiphon for Trinity Sunday).

The priest turns to the people and says:
P. The Lord be with you. *(Dominus vobiscum.)*
S. And with thy spirit. *(Et cum spiritu tuo.)*

Having purified the chalice and covered it with the veil, the priest retires to the Epistle side of the altar and reads from the Missal a short verse which is called the **Communion Antiphon.** It consists usually of a single Scriptural verse and varies with each Sunday and feast day. It is called the **Communion Antiphon,** or simply the **Communion,** because it was formerly chanted by the choir while the priest distributed Communion to the faithful. It is a canticle of praise and joy, a canticle of a jubilant soul which has been made partaker of the holy Mysteries. After Our Lord had communicated His Body and Blood to His Apostles, the Scripture says: "And a hymn being said, they went out unto Mount Olivet." (*Matt.* 26:30).

The Postcommunion

The priest reads the last prayers from the Missal.

P. Let us pray. May the receiving of this Sacrament, O Lord our God, and the confession of the holy and eternal Trinity and its undivided Unity, profit us for the health of body and soul; through our

Lord Jesus Christ, Thy Son, Who liveth and reigneth with Thee in the unity of the Holy Ghost, God, world without end. (Postcommunion for Trinity Sunday).
S. Amen.

When the priest has finished reading the anthem which is called the **Communion Antiphon,** he returns to the center, kisses the altar and again salutes the people with the familiar greeting, ***"Dominus vobiscum"***—**"The Lord be with you**." It must be borne in mind that this part of the Mass is an act of thanksgiving due to the Almighty. By saluting the people here, the priest gives expression to his desire that the Lord Whom they have received, either in reality or in spirit, may always abide with them, according to His own promise: "He that eateth My Flesh, and drinketh My Blood, abideth in Me, and I in him." (*John* 6:57).

When the server, in the name of the congregation, has replied to the priest's greeting with the words, ***"Et cum spiritu tuo"***—**"And with thy spirit,"** the priest returns again to the Missal. With arms extended he reads the prayer known as the **Postcommunion.** The Latin word ***"post"*** means **"after."** Because this prayer is recited **after** the **Communion** it is called the **Postcommunion.** In number and subject the Postcommunion corresponds with the **Collect** and **Secret.** If three **Collects** are recited (before the Epistle), the **Secret** and the **Postcommunion** will also be three in number. In the Postcommunion, mention is always made of the Body and Blood of Christ which has been received. The Postcommunion may be regarded as an act of thanksgiving. "All whatsoever you do in word or in work, do all in the name of the Lord Jesus Christ, giving thanks to God and the Father by Him." (*Col.* 3:17).

Ite, Missa Est

Returning to the center of the altar, the priest faces the congregation.

P. The Lord be with you. ***(Dominus vobiscum.)***
S. And with thy spirit. ***(Et cum spiritu tuo.)***
P. Go, it is the dismissal. ***(Ite, missa est.)***
S. Thanks be to God. ***(Deo Gratias.)***

The **Postcommunion** being ended, the priest returns to the center and again salutes the faithful with the words, **"The Lord be with you"**—as if he would say: "Although you are about to depart from the house of God, may He accompany you with His grace whithersoever you may go." And the people make answer, saying through the server: **"And with thy spirit,"** praying that the Lord may ever guide and direct their well-wisher aright.

Still facing the congregation, the priest says, ***"Ite, missa est"***—**"Go, it is the dismissal."** In olden days the time for the dismissal was announced to the congregation by the deacon. This is still done today at a Solemn High Mass. To this announcement the congregation answers through the server, ***"Deo gratias"***—**"Thanks be to God."** This is said in a spirit of gratitude, for eternal thanks are due to the Almighty for sacrificing His only Son for the Redemption of mankind, which Sacrifice is renewed in every Mass. Thanks are also due to God for having given us the grace to be present at so wholesome a sacrifice.

On days which have a character of penance or sadness, this versicle *("Ite, missa est")* is replaced by the words, ***"Benedicamus Domino"***—**"Let us bless the Lord."**

Formerly it was customary for the faithful to remain in the church after the Mass on days of fasting and to spend some time in prayer. Hence the dismissal was not announced, but rather an invitation to praise the Lord was extended. It will be noted that on the Sundays during Advent and Lent, when the priest wears violet vestments, the **Benedicamus Domino** is recited in place of the **Ite, Missa Est.** The rule was gradually established that the congregation should be solemnly dismissed with the words, ***"Ite, missa est,"*** on those days on which the **Gloria** was sung. So the idea obtained that ***"Ite, missa est"*** implies a festal Mass.

In Requiem Masses, instead of the **Ite, Missa Est** the priest uses the versicle, ***"Requiescant in pace"*—"May they rest in peace."** To this the server answers, ***"Amen."*** When the priest says ***"Ite, missa est,"*** he faces the people, because the dismissal is announced to them. When he says ***"Benedicamus Domino"*—"Let us bless the Lord,"** he faces the tabernacle, where Our Lord is present in a special manner. When he says ***"Requiescant in pace,"*** he does not face the congregation, because mention is being made of the absent brethren.

The Placeat Tibi and the Blessing

The priest invokes the blessing of God.

Bowing down before the altar, the priest says:

May the homage of my service be pleasing to Thee, O Holy Trinity, and grant that the Sacrifice which I, though unworthy, have offered up in the sight of Thy Majesty, may be acceptable to Thee, and through Thy mercy be a propitiation for me and all those for whom I have offered it. Through Christ our Lord. Amen.

Blessing the people, he says:

P. May Almighty God bless you, ✠ the Father, the Son, and the Holy Ghost.

S. Amen.

After the server has responded to the ***"Ite, missa est,"*** the priest again turns to the altar. Mindful of the great action he has performed, he bows down his head in humility and says the following prayer: ***"Placeat tibi, Sancta Trinitas"*****—"May the homage of my service,"** etc. In this prayer the priest acknowledges that he never would have presumed to perform this service had it not been in obedience to the command of the Saviour. He asks that God, in His infinite goodness, may overlook his unworthiness and grant a blessing to himself and to all for whom the Sacrifice has been offered.

Upon concluding the preceding prayer, the priest again kisses the altar. This is done out of reverence for the great Sacrifice which took place upon the altar, and also to indicate that through this Sacrifice we are brought into closer communion with Christ, Who is symbolized by the altar. It is from this union with Christ that the priest, as the dispenser of the mysteries of God, receives the power to impart to the faithful, by means of the Sign of the Cross, the blessings of the Redemption.

Raising his eyes and hands toward Heaven, whence flows every good gift, the priest now prays: **"May Almighty God bless you"** (then turning toward the people and making the Sign of the Cross over them, he continues and says), **"the Father, the Son, and the Holy Ghost."** The server answers, **"Amen."**

The blessing of a man venerable for his age or position or sanctity has, from the beginning of the world, been asked and received with gratitude by the man of faith, for "the continual prayer of a just man availeth much." (*James* 5:16). In the Old Law, the priests were commanded to bless the people: "Thus shall you bless the children of Israel, and you shall say to them: The Lord bless thee and keep thee. . . . And they shall invoke My Name upon the children of Israel, and I will bless them." (*Num.* 6:23-27). Christ blessed His Apostles before He ascended into Heaven: "And lifting up His hands, He blessed them." (*Luke* 24:50). A ceremony so conformable to nature, and practiced by Christ Himself, has with reason been adopted by the Church in her ceremonial. At no time could it be exercised with more propriety than at the conclusion of the Mass, before the people leave the house of God for their homes. As a father blesses, so the priest dismisses his spiritual children with a blessing. As the Apostles, after receiving the blessing of Christ on Mt. Olivet, "went back into Jerusalem with great joy . . . praising and blessing God" (*Luke* 24:52), so the people, after assisting at Mass and having received the blessing of Christ's Church, should return to their respective occupations with joy, giving praise to God.

The Last Gospel

The priest reads the Last Gospel.

P. The Lord be with you. *(Dominus vobiscum.)*
S. And with thy spirit. *(Et cum spiritu tuo.)*
P. The beginning of the Holy Gospel according to St. John. *(Initium sancti Evangelii secundum Ioannem.)*

S. Glory be to Thee, O Lord. ***(Gloria tibi, Domine.)***

P. In the beginning was the Word, and the Word was with God, and the Word was God: the same was in the beginning with God. All things were made by Him, and without Him was made nothing that was made. In Him was life, and the life was the light of men: and the light shineth in darkness, and the darkness did not comprehend it. There was a man, one sent from God, whose name was John. This man came for a witness, to give testimony of the Light, that all men might believe through Him. He was not the Light, but was to give testimony of the Light. That was the true Light, which enlighteneth every man that cometh into this world. He was in the world, and the world was made by Him, and the world knew Him not. He came unto His own, and His own received Him not. But as many as received Him, He gave them power to be made the sons of God: to them that believe in His Name, who are born not of blood, nor of the will of the flesh, nor of the will of man, but of God. (*Here all genuflect:*) AND THE WORD WAS MADE FLESH, and dwelt among us: and we saw His glory, the glory as of the Only-begotten of the Father, full of grace and truth.

S. Thanks be to God. ***(Deo Gratias.)***

Having imparted the blessing, the celebrant proceeds to the Gospel side (left side) of the altar. Before beginning to read the Gospel, he says: **"The Lord be with you."** To this the server gives the usual response: **"And with thy spirit."** By this greeting the attention of the faithful is aroused to listen devoutly to the Gospel reading. Then with his thumb the priest makes the

Sign of the Cross upon the altar card or upon the altar, saying: **"The beginning of the holy Gospel according to St. John."** To this the server makes answer: **"Glory be to Thee, O Lord."** By making the Sign of the Cross upon the altar card or upon the altar, the priest indicates that the Gospel is the word of Christ in testimony of which Christ gave up His life on the Cross. At the words **"Glory be to Thee, O Lord,"** the priest makes the Sign of the Cross with his thumb on his forehead, on his lips and on his heart, begging of God grace to know, to profess and to love His teaching.

With folded hands the priest now reads from the altar card the first fourteen verses of the first chapter of the Gospel according to St. John. This reading, in the course of time, was added to the Eucharistic service on account of the great reverence the early Christians entertained for this portion of the Gospel and because it contains a summary of the benefits of which we are made partakers through Christ's Sacrifice. The service was introduced by the prayer of the priest: **"Send forth Thy light and Thy truth!"** It could not be concluded in a more becoming manner than with the words: **"AND THE WORD WAS MADE FLESH, and dwelt among us; and we saw His glory, the glory as of the Only-begotten of the Father, full of grace and truth."** At the words **"AND THE WORD WAS MADE FLESH,"** the priest and people kneel on one knee in token of adoration of the mystery of the Incarnation, which is expressed by these words, and to indicate that the Son of God came from Heaven to earth. When the priest has finished the reading of this Gospel, the server answers, ***"Deo gratias"***—**"Thanks be to God."** These are the last words of the Mass.

For some Masses, the Church has appointed another

Gospel reading in place of the beginning of the Gospel according to St. John. When another Gospel is to be substituted, the priest does not close the Missal after finishing the Postcommunion. When the Missal is left open after the Postcommunion, the server knows that the Last Gospel will not be the Gospel according to St. John, but that some other Gospel will be read in its stead, and therefore he carries the Missal over to the Gospel side of the altar.

Leaving the Sanctuary

At a Low Mass, after the priest reads the Last Gospel, the priest and congregation recite the Prayers after Low Mass. (See p. 186). These being completed, the people stand as the priest ascends the altar steps to pick up the chalice, veil and burse from the altar, while the server retrieves the biretta from the table on the Epistle side of the Sanctuary. After descending the steps, the priest stands facing the altar while he places the biretta on his head. The priest and server genuflect together in adoration of Our Lord in the tabernacle. The priest then turns to the left and leaves the Sanctuary, preceded by the server.

Mass is now finished. The people may leave the church or may kneel down and continue to pray silently. Each person, as he leaves, genuflects toward Christ in the tabernacle as an act of adoration. A red *sanctuary lamp* burns near the tabernacle. A holy silence reigns in the church at all times, for any church in which the Blessed Sacrament is reserved is the House of God.

Chapter 5

After Mass

PRAYERS AFTER LOW MASS

For the Church in Russia. Prescribed by Pope Leo XIII (in 1884) and by Pope Pius XI (in 1934), with three-fold aspiration at the end prescribed by Pope St. Pius X (in 1904). These prayers are led by the priest, kneeling on one of the altar steps. The congregation responds.

The Hail Mary

(Recite three times.)

P. **Hail Mary, full of grace, the Lord is with thee; blessed art thou among women, and blessed is the fruit of thy womb, Jesus.**

All: **Holy Mary, Mother of God, pray for us sinners, now and at the hour of our death. Amen.**

P. **Hail Holy Queen,**

All: **Mother of mercy, our life, our sweetness and our hope. To thee do we cry, poor banished children of Eve. To thee do we send up our sighs, mourning and weeping in this valley of tears. Turn then, most gracious advocate, thine eyes of mercy towards us. And after this our exile, show unto us the blessed fruit of thy womb, Jesus. O clement, O loving, O sweet Virgin Mary,**

P. Pray for us, O holy Mother of God,
All: That we may be made worthy of the promises of Christ.

Let us Pray.

P. O God, our refuge and our strength, look down in mercy on Thy people who cry to Thee; and through the intercession of the glorious and immaculate Virgin Mary, Mother of God, of St. Joseph her spouse, of Thy holy apostles Peter and Paul, and of all the saints, in mercy and goodness hear our prayers for the conversion of sinners, and for the liberty and exaltation of our holy Mother the Church. Through the same Christ our Lord.
All: Amen.

P. St. Michael the Archangel,
All: defend us in battle; be our defense against the wickedness and snares of the devil. May God rebuke him, we humbly pray, and do thou, O prince of the heavenly host, by the power of God cast into Hell Satan and all the evil spirits, who wander through the world seeking the ruin of souls. Amen.

(Three times:)
P. Most Sacred Heart of Jesus,
All: Have mercy on us.

AFTER MASS

It is all over now, and you may go back into the busy street and into your own homes. Nothing has changed since you left it all an hour or so ago. Only this has happened: You have stood in the presence of the living God; you have shared in the most sacred and solemn action that it is possible to conceive as taking place on this earth. "He was in the world, and the world knew Him not." Perhaps until today you were among the number of those who knew Him not. You know Him now. Pray that God may give you grace and courage to follow Him Whom you know to have the words of everlasting life, so that one day you may be numbered among the "sons of God."

"In Every Place There Is Sacrifice"

Fr. F. X. Lasance

"Did you ever think that the Holy Sacrifice of the Mass is being offered in some part of the world every hour of your life? When it is midnight in New York, Masses are beginning in the churches of Italy. There ancient altars, at which Saints have knelt, are lit up with tapers, and the Vicar of Christ and thousands of priests are lifting holy hands up to Heaven. A little later and the bells of a thousand towers in France begin to sprinkle the air with holy sounds; and in every city, town and hamlet, kneeling crowds adore the chastening hand of God and pray for sinners who despise His ordinances.

"Chivalric and religious Spain catches the echoes, and when it is one a.m. in New York, offers the great Sacrifice in countless splendid churches. And then Catholic Ireland, the "Island of Saints," which has during many centuries suffered for the Faith, rallies anew around the altars it would never forsake. At two o'clock and after, the priests of the islands of the Atlantic—perhaps the Cape Verde—white-robed and stoled and wearing the great cross on their shoulders, bend before the tabernacle. An hour later a courageous missionary lifts up the chalice of salvation on the ice-bound coast of Greenland.

"At half-past four the sacred lamps twinkle through the fogs of Newfoundland; and at five, Nova Scotia's industrious population begins the day by attending Mass. And now all the Canadian churches and chapels grow radiant as the faithful people—the habitant of the country, the devout citizen, the consecrated nun, and the innocent—hasten to unite their prayers around the sanctuary where the priest is awaiting them. At six, how many souls are flocking to the churches of New York, eager to begin the day of labor with the holiest act of religion! Many young people, too, gather around the altar at a later hour, like the fresh flowers open with the morning, and offer their dewy fragrance to Heaven. An hour later the bells of Missouri and Louisiana are ringing; and at eight, Mexico, true to her faith, bends before her glittering altars. At nine the devout tribes of Oregon follow their beloved black gown to their gay chapels, and California awhile loosens its grasp on its gold to think of the treasure that rust doth not corrupt.

"And when the Angelus bell is ringing at noon in New York, the unbloody Sacrifice is being offered up in the islands of the Pacific, where there are generous souls laboring for our dear Lord. And so the bells are ringing on, on, over the waters, and one taper after another catches the light of faith, making glad all the isles of the sea. At two the zealous missionaries of Australia are murmuring with haste, eager for the coming of Our Lord: *"Introibo ad altare Dei."* And all the spicy islands of the East catch the sweet sounds, one after another, till at four in the afternoon China proves there are many souls who are worthy of the name of *celestial* by their rapt devotion at the early rite. Then in Tibet there is many a modest chapel where the missionary distributes the Bread of Life to a crowd of hungry souls.

"At six the altars of Hindustan, where St. Francis Xavier ministered, are arrayed with their flowers and lamps and the sacred vessels, and unwearied priests are hastening to fortify their souls before Him Who is their life and their strength. At nine in Siberia, where many a poor Catholic exile from Poland has no other solace from his woes but the foot of the altar and the Bread of Heaven. During the hours when New York is gay with parties and balls and theatrical amusements, the holiest of rites is going on in the Indian Ocean and among the sable tribes of Africa, whose souls are so dear to the Saviour Who once died for all. At eleven in Jerusalem, the Holy City over which Jesus wept, where He wrought so many miracles, where He suffered and offered Himself a sacrifice for the whole world.

"When midnight sounds again in New York, the silver bells are tinkling again in every chancel in Rome. And so it goes on; the divine Host is constantly rising like the sun in its course around the earth. Thus are fulfilled the words of the prophet Malachias [1:11]: 'From the rising of the sun even to the going down thereof, My name is great among the Gentiles; and in every place there is sacrifice, and there is offered to My name a clean oblation: for My name is great among the Gentiles, saith the Lord of hosts.'"

"Not an instant of time passes that a Mass is not offered, and the Host not adored. Talk of an Empire on which the sun never sets, of the British reveille drum ever beating as our planet revolves on its axis and day chases night around the globe; what is that to the unending oblation of the Catholic Church? What moment is not a priest's voice uttering *'Te igitur, clementissime Pater!'* What moment is not counted by the bell which announces the silent and invisible coming of their God to prostrate adorers in some quiet sanctuary, in Europe, or in Asia, or in America, in the Atlantic cities or in the woods of Oregon, in the Alps or on the Andes, on the vast terra firma all along the Meridians or on the scattered islands of the sea?"
—Webster (*Knickerbockers' Mag.,* p. 638, vol. 38, 1851).

About the Author

Msgr. George J. Moorman
1883-1979

Msgr. George Moorman was born in Decatur County, Indiana on October 9, 1883, and he lived almost his entire life in Indiana. He attended St. Meinrad Seminary and was ordained by Bishop Herman J. Alerding of Fort Wayne on June 13, 1908 at the Cathedral of the Immaculate Conception.

During a priesthood of more than 70 years, Fr. George Moorman served as pastor at several parishes. For a time, he was associate editor of *Our Sunday Visitor,* beginning in 1914. Fr. Moorman volunteered as an army chaplain in 1917 and served during World War I. He was commissioned as 1st Lt. Chaplain. He was appointed Dean of the South Bend deanery in 1930 and was invested as a Papal Chamberlain in 1940.

Retiring from active duty in 1959, Msgr. Moorman lived in Greensburg, Indiana until illness at the end of his life brought him to Sacred Heart home, Avila. There he died on July 5, 1979 at the age of 95, being at the time the oldest priest in the Diocese of Fort Wayne-South Bend.

Father Raymond Moorman, nephew of Msgr. Moorman, was the principal celebrant of a "Mass of the Resurrection" concelebrated by three bishops and some 40 priests at the Cathedral of the Immaculate Conception, Fort Wayne on July 9. A funeral Mass, followed by burial, took place the following day at Millhousen, Indiana, the town in which Msgr. Moorman had attended St. Mary's School in his youth.

The above is summarized from an article that appeared in the July 15, 1979 issue of *The Harmonizer,* diocesan newspaper of the Diocese of Fort Wayne-South Bend. Grateful acknowledgments to the diocesan archivist.

TAN Books was founded in 1967 to preserve the spiritual, intellectual and liturgical traditions of the Catholic Church. At a critical moment in history TAN kept alive the great classics of the Faith and drew many to the Church. In 2008 TAN was acquired by Saint Benedict Press. Today TAN continues its mission to a new generation of readers.

From its earliest days TAN has published a range of booklets that teach and defend the Faith. Through partnerships with organizations, apostolates, and mission-minded individuals, well over 10 million TAN booklets have been distributed.

More recently, TAN has expanded its publishing with the launch of Catholic calendars and daily planners—as well as Bibles, fiction, and multimedia products through its sister imprints Catholic Courses (catholiccourses.com) and Saint Benedict Press (saintbenedictpress.com).

Today TAN publishes over 500 titles in the areas of theology, prayer, devotions, doctrine, Church history, and the lives of the saints. TAN books are published in multiple languages and found throughout the world in schools, parishes, bookstores and homes.